LANCASHIRE
BADGER GROUP

WORKING TOGETHER, PROTECTING BADGERS

PO Box 58, Lancaster, LA1 5AF.

www.lancashirebadgergroup.org.uk

1st Published in 2016

© Andrew M Parr 2016

Picture credits and copyright:

Fig: 1-5, 7- 9, 12-15, 17-20, 22-23, 27, 33, 39: A. Parr©

Fig: 6, 10-11, 16, 21, 34: SWWR / A. Parr©

Appendix: 4, 5 A. Parr©

Fig: 28-32, 35, 38: SWWR©

Appendix: 1, 2, 3 SWWR©

Fig: 24-26: Derek Barry©

Fig: 36-37: Sara Cowen©

ISBN 978-0- 9956167-0- 7

This handbook was printed using FSC certified paper & vegetable inks

The printing of this handbook was generously sponsored by:

Mark and Barbara Martin

All proceeds from the sale of this handbook will be used by Lancashire Badger Group as part of a children's wildlife educational programme

Designed and set by: madebymason.co.uk & wearelighten.co.uk

THE REHABILITATOR'S

&

BADGER ENTHUSIAST'S

HANDBOOK

Returning badger cubs (*Meles meles*) to the natal sett following short term rehabilitation

Andy Parr

CONTENTS:

FOREWORD

I have been involved with badgers and badger conservation since the early 1990's. My passion and interest in wildlife was kindled at an early age; my father was an entomologist and lecturer at Salford University and as a child I often accompanied him on local field trips. Badgers were an "exotic species" in 1960's Salford (and probably still are today) so I concentrated on caterpillars, hawk-moths and dissecting tawny owl pellets! At the age of 9 my Auntie Joan gave me my first badger book; A Forest by Night by Fred J Speakman, the seed was sown.

I studied horticulture at Lancashire College of Agriculture and then set up (in partnership) a landscaping and horticultural contracting business, though these days my work is mainly focused as a surveyor and part-time ecologist.

I became involved with the Lancashire Badger Group when I read in a local newspaper about the conviction of a man for digging badgers and then realised this sett was located in a wood near to where I lived. The following day I found the sett in question and a very forthright badger group member who "interrogated" me over my interest in the badgers. The man in question was Clive Walsh, a very knowledgeable and passionate badger enthusiast. Without his tenacity and badger like determination, there would be far fewer badgers in many upland areas of Bolton and Blackburn today. Over the next few years we became very good friends and I learned a great deal about badger watching, ecology and conservation from this true conservationist. I joined the Lancashire Badger Group and soon became part of a team that specialised in capping vulnerable setts with steel mesh and thus protecting them from badger diggers. I also began a process of monitoring 'at risk' setts with the installation of covert cameras.

In 2007 I moved from Lancashire to the South West of England and became involved with the Somerset Badger Group and Secret World Wildlife Rescue (SWWR). In 2010 I was offered a position as the Wildlife Release Manager at Secret World; where my interest in badgers and other species was allowed to grow.

I became aware of the huge pressure of limited release sites available for rehabilitated badger cubs and where possible the need to limit the number of badger cubs being admitted into SWWR and other rescue centres. Whilst working as the Release Manager I took the opportunity to explore techniques in returning "orphaned or abandoned" cubs back to the natal sett. This handbook encompasses the work and findings of badger cub natal returns.

I currently volunteer with the Somerset Badger Group and SWWR with badger and other wildlife related matters.

I would like to thank the numerous badger groups who contributed with data, the staff and volunteers at Secret World Wildlife Rescue for their support in this research and especially Pauline Kidner (Founder), Simon Kidner, Elizabeth Mullineaux, Adrian Coward, Vanessa Mason and Sara Cowen (Animal Care Manager); Sara was at the forefront in supporting this work and was a vital part in ensuring all badger cubs entering the centre and those requiring attention in the field received the appropriate response.

Finally, many thanks to my wife Alison. Without her support, assistance in natal returns and passion for wildlife, this handbook would not have been possible.

Andy Parr

CHAPTER 1:
INTRODUCTION

The rescue of a cub or adult badger should only be undertaken by a trained/experienced person with a sound understanding of badgers and badger ecology.

Both a cub and adult badger have the ability to inflict serious injury if rescued incorrectly. If you do not have this experience or are unsure, then contact your local wildlife rescue centre or The Badger Trust for a list of local badger groups who will be able to assist you.

Not all juvenile animals admitted to rescue centres are true orphans and it is frequently publicised that fledglings are taken to rescue centres when in fact many are not abandoned. As with larger mammals such as fawns, fox and otter cubs, badger cubs are also rescued in the wild and either considered orphaned or abandoned and in need of rehabilitation. However, this may not be the case. What is clear is that once mobile, a badger cub has the ability to forage long distances from the sett and potentially become temporally separated from the sett or its social group. Many counties (in the UK) have dedicated badger groups that respond to badgers and cubs in distress. For these reasons it is not surprising that badger cubs are widely presented to rescue centres throughout the UK.

Exactly how many of these badger cubs are true orphans and in need of Long Term Rehabilitation (LTR) is impossible to state with any accuracy and it is reasonable to surmise that this may vary from year to year depending upon prevailing environmental conditions. However, based on my observations and experiences, the number of true orphans could be around 40-50%. This then leaves approximately 50-60% of cubs that could fit the criteria for a potential return to the natal sett.

There is a note of caution in that just because a cub is thought suitable for a natal return there may be influencing factors that preclude a release. This will be discussed in further detail especially within 'Case Studies'.

There are many reasons why a badger cub could be brought into a rescue centre, these include:

Table I
I) Injured
a) Road Traffic Collision (RTC)
b) Fall (cliff/high wall)
c) Dog or wild animal attack
2) Sickness/Disease
a) Natural causes
b) Poison
3) Found in someone's possession (illegally)
4) Extreme variants in the weather
a) Flooding
b) Excessive dry weather
c) Lack of food or water
5) Detached (lost) from the sow or social group/sett
6) Trapped
7) Found next to a dead or injured sow
8) Disturbance
a) Dog entering a sett and removing the cub(s)
b) Persecution
c) Sett uncovered during earthworks or demolition or moving a long term temporary structure such as a cabin/container/building
9) Rejected by the sow or social group

This is by no means an exhaustive list but provides a comprehensive insight into the variety and complexity of animals entering rescue centres.

There are clear situations where a cub will have to be admitted for LTR and it may then be beneficial for the animal to be released in a new social group (formed with similar cubs) later in the season [1].

A responsible LTR programme will typically consist of the following protocol:

Table 2
1. Blood testing on three occasions for bovine tuberculosis (bTB) with those animals returning a positive test being euthanised
2. Vaccination (when available) with the Bacillus Calmette-Guérin vaccine (badger BCG vaccine)
3. Forming a new social group 3-8 individuals
4. Forming a viable male to female ratio within this social group
5. Procuring a suitable release site that will accommodate the cubs? Key aspects include:
a. Low existing (resident) badger numbers
b. Good feeding habitat throughout the year
c. Site not subject to excesses in weather extremes; flooding or very sandy free draining soil - drought
d. Low persecution
e. Conflict with people
f. Proximity of major roads, electric rails or a very busy railway
g. Potential to expand and construct new setts naturally
6. Locating a suitable disused (donor) sett or the construction of a permanent artificial sett
7. Undertaking a soft release programme with long term support feeding

It should be the role of wildlife centres, rescuers, rehabilitators and badger groups to ensure that only those animals that are in true need of rescuing and rehabilitation should be admitted into a centre for LTR. Every endeavour should be undertaken to establish the circumstances as to why this animal has been rescued and the question asked; is there any good reason why it should not be returned quickly to the wild?

Every wildlife rescue situation is different, whether it is environmental, single or multiple animals, health issues or conflicting view points from those people involved in the rescue and care of the cub.

Benefits associated with this approach include:

Table 3
1. Reduced numbers of badger cubs being admitted into the centre
2. Release site resources can be targeted at genuine orphaned cubs
3. If cubs are supported within their natal range then this would negate the need for bTB blood tests and the potential issues relating to false positives/euthanasia sometimes associated with the test
4. Reduced potential conflict with some farmers/landowners when introducing badgers into a new release site
5. Potential cost savings compared with the widely adopted LTR method
6. Cub has the benefits of being raised naturally in the wild and the ability to learn life skills from the sow
7. A sustainable lower carbon approach to wildlife rehabilitation

Problems associated with this approach:

Table 4
1. The risk of releasing a badger cub in the wrong territory, especially when dealing with cubs in small territories or setts of two different social groups located close to each other, thus creating potential welfare concerns
2. Accidental overlooking/misdiagnosis of hidden health issues relating to a cub
3. How to overcome the emotive nature of "abandoned" cubs and extract the influencing factors behind each abandonment
4. How to overcome the knee jerk reaction when people can automatically perceive all cubs are abandoned and bring them into a rehabilitation centre
5. Potential for making a mistake and not fully understanding the complexity of a cub release resulting in welfare issues [2]. Examples would be releasing a pre-weaned cub without establishing the lactating sow is alive, healthy and prepared to engage with the cub, or releasing a cub following treatment for dehydration (when the weather was still dry) and not providing a support package of water and food at the sett

CHAPTER 2:
RESEARCH

I approached as many wildlife rescue centres I could locate and all the badger groups nationally, asking for any experiences in returning badger cubs to their natal sett. There were very few returns to this request. Those that did reply with extensive accounts were in the main from badger groups, with one group having undertaken two separate returns; Mid-Derbyshire Badger Group. Somerset Badger Group also successfully returned and support fed a cub at the sett.

With the case of the Somerset Badger Group, Adrian Coward (then Chair of the group) was able to positively identify the cub during and beyond the support feeding process. There were on the whole no means for the other groups or individuals to verify the ultimate outcome of the cubs returned to the sett, though the feedback was considered to be positive.

There are a few references within books regarding cubs that have been returned including a detailed account by Michael Clark; Badgers 1989 (page 78). However, most accounts written or verbal are anecdotal references with limited factual information on the ultimate survival of the cub. The return of a cub to the natal sett is quite clearly not a new idea but one that I feel has become overlooked with the advent of dedicated and specialised wildlife rescue centres.

The information and case studies within this book are based upon research undertaken over a 5 year period whilst working and volunteering at SWWR, as a Wildlife Release Manager. Of particular interest were the circumstances as to how badger cubs ended up within a rescue centre, with attention focused on the following data:

- Health/Condition

- Circumstances of rescue

- Age of the cub

Where appropriate I attended the site and undertook a survey.

It was important to develop a clear understanding of why cubs come into rescue centres and whether any of these cubs could be prevented from going through LTR. As an alternative, could they be released (following treatment) back into the territory/natal sett from which they originated and if so, how could this be achieved with the animal's welfare paramount?

RESEARCH OBJECTIVES

The core of the research was to establish various methods of assessing "orphaned" badger cubs and if applicable develop a release strategy that would allow the selection of the appropriate release package for each cub. It was envisaged that with experience it would be possible to build up a database that would highlight similarities in types of rescues and therefore make informed decisions based on outcomes of previous releases.

Attempting to return a cub to the natal sett presented varying challenges and different approaches were required depending primarily upon the age of the cub. On that basis the focus of the research depended upon categorising the age/development of the individual animal. For this a standard reference (age) chart was used see Appendix 1. Also see Appendix 1A Estimating the age of badger cubs: Photographs.

The focus of the research was divided into the following categories:

Table 5
1. Cubs pre-weaned:
immobile and mobile cubs
2. Cubs weaned:
including support feeding
3. Rehabilitation – duration:
establishing the duration a cub can be held in a rehabilitation facility and then successfully released

CUB AND RESEARCH PROTOCOLS

A protocol for assessing and prioritising badger cubs was developed; see Appendix 2. This protocol was also devised so that there was a standardised approach to calls relating to cubs in difficulties; this would enable those manning the phone to ask the appropriate questions regarding the cub and its condition/circumstances. This would then ensure that the correct response/rescue could be implemented for that individual animal. Wherever possible and recognising the safeguards in Appendix 2, cub(s) were kept in-situ until the site had been surveyed by someone with badger experience, usually from a badger group.

Guidance on the treatment of orphaned cubs was compiled; see Appendix 3. This provided initial and essential information on dealing with badger cub casualties.

The principal objective was that, wherever possible, a cub should be returned to its natal sett and monitored live via a camera during the release. This would provide the opportunity to observe the reactions of the cub and sow/adults during the process. This would give the option to allow the release to go ahead or step in and halt the release if there were any concerns. For this process the term Monitored Natal Return (MNR) was used. It was of the utmost importance that cubs would not simply be left at the sett and assumed all was well. It was considered that to validate this approach the cub's behaviour at the sett had to be observed and where appropriate the cub/sow relationship.

A protocol was developed for the potential release of cubs to the natal sett; see Appendix 4 (Key points) with clear differences between the age group of the cubs. Cubs that were pre-weaned and thus still dependent upon a sow for food would only be released if an adult badger (lactating sow) engaged positively with the cub. There is a legal responsibility in this matter [2]. Once a juvenile animal is taken into care, it should not be released if it is unable to fend for itself in the wild.

Cubs that are weaned offer more flexibility in this matter, but the risks of a cub straying into a neighbouring territory increase as a cub becomes older and thus more mobile. In these cases general site recognition (of its environment) by the cub or a positive reaction with any adult badger at the sett were of greater significance.

A cub entering the centre when they are more mature (late June onwards) could be considered for release back into a territory without the sett being located, providing there were no extenuating circumstances such as severe hierarchal or territorial wounds (fight wounds). It transpired that with this group, most of these cases centred around cubs becoming trapped or as a result of a minor RTC.

Badgers are territorial and a cub straying into a neighbouring territory may very well be subjected to aggression. It is imperative for the welfare of a cub (of any age) that safeguards are in place for the cub before a release is undertaken. Where a cub has shown signs of fight related injuries (badger) these can be inflicted by badgers from a neighbouring social group and sometimes from the same social group. These cubs should be monitored closely during a release and the reactions of badgers at the release site observed for levels of aggression before allowing a release to go ahead. Play fighting amongst cubs and some adults can cause minor injuries and these should not be used as a barrier when considering a release, as this is part of the badger's natural behaviour. Evidence of sustained aggression should be treated with caution.

Fight wounds on adult badgers and sub-adults tend to be associated with the rump, ears and neck. Juvenile badgers can present the fore-mentioned injuries but also on other parts of the body, which can make it difficult to differentiate from that of a dog attack.

Follow up monitoring should be undertaken with the aid of a micro-chip (licenced procedure) implanted within the cub which is identical to a domestic cat/dog chip. This should then allow the logging of the chip with the installation of a micro-chip reader; Radio Frequency Identification (RFID) at the natal sett. Radio tracking via collar transmitters is not suitable, as there is a potential welfare issue associated with the fitting of collars to juvenile (rapidly developing) animals within the wild.

A general protocol dealing with badger cub rescues is detailed within Appendix 5, (Check list for dealing with a rescued badger cub).

LICENCE

Following consultation with Natural England (NE) and the Countryside Council for Wales (CCW) a 3 year licence was obtained from NE and a 2 year licence from CCW. These licences permitted the marking (micro-chipping) of badgers and the fitting of the RFID/antenna at a sett entrance, providing a strict protocol was observed:

RFID Installation protocol:

Table 6
1. All equipment must be thoroughly cleaned before each installation
2. The equipment must not harm or interfere with the badgers movement
3. The equipment should only be installed/removed 4 hours before sunset, to reduce scent disturbance
4. Slight remodeling of the sett entrance aperture was allowed to ensure a close and secure fit of the antenna
5. The licences permitted the installation of the RFID equipment at a sett without prior notification to either body. This allowed us to respond quickly to the release of a cub(s)

A licence is not required to return a cub to the natal sett providing the process does not overly disturb the resident badgers, which if done correctly should not create any such issues.

A licence is required for marking, ringing or tagging a badger [3]. It would be sensible for anyone involved in the rehabilitation of badgers to contact NE or the CCW to determine if any of their activities in the treatment and care of badgers fall within licensable works.

EQUIPMENT INCLUDING FUR CLIPPING

MICRO-CHIP

Micro-id mini-chips (tags) were used, as these were approximately 44% smaller than a traditional chip. A traditional chip measures 12mm long and 2.12mm wide whereas the mini-chip measures 8mm long and 1.4mm wide. These chips are also considered less invasive as the majority of the target animals would be juveniles and the sterile single use was more suitable for use in the field.

Although it is permissible to micro-chip a badger cub below the age of 5-6 weeks old (under licence) my personal feelings are that this process should not be undertaken with cubs of this age, unless there are good welfare grounds to support this action.

The implanting of the micro-chip was found to be critical for the successful reading of the chip with a fixed antenna/RFID system in the field. The chip was implanted between the shoulder blades in the dorsal midline (as per the international standard for these mammals) [4]. It was imperative that this chip was placed in a cranial-caudal (head to tail) direction between the shoulder blades (rather than at right angles to this line). This ensured a regular and strong logging of the chip.

In tests, a bare micro-chip placed in the hand and then passed through the antenna sideways, failed to register. As the chip position was changed to one of passing through the antenna end first it registered immediately. This obviously had implications for chips that may occasionally migrate in the body and would possibly explain that on rare occasions the badger caught in the camera trap visually identified was our "target" but failed to register on the RFID reader. Consultation with the micro-chip supplier revealed that it was thought the smaller mini-chip was less prone to migrate in the body than a standard size chip, though it must be pointed out that micro-chip migration (in any size) is a rare occurrence. Other types of micro-chip were tested and all were found to be similar in performance with a fixed antenna system (as opposed to a typical hand held scanner).

The need to record micro-chip numbers is crucial in post release monitoring. It must be remembered that domestic pets and livestock will in most cases have micro-chip implants or ear tags. Unless you have a clear record of implanted chips, non-target species could cause problems with confirming the presence of your badger.

RFID (RADIO FREQUENCY IDENTIFICATION)

The RFID reader consisted of a rigid resin rectangular antenna measuring 250mm x 300mm which the badger had to pass through to register. The data recorded included the unique micro-chip number, date, time and a reference number. The equipment was powered by a 12v/72ah leisure battery with an operational life span of approximately 14 days. The equipment was capable of logging thousands of data entries over the installation period.

There were three methods deployed in using the RFID reader:

Table 7
1. Placing the antenna on a well-used sett entrance
2. Placing the antenna on a feeding tube/station see Fig. 1
3. Placing the antenna on a well-used path near to the sett

It was found that if the sett was of a multi-hole configuration, then it could be hit or miss whether the target badger was recorded. In many cases placing food regularly within a secured section of 300mm dia. pipe (feeding tube) and placing the antenna on one end of the pipe, ensured very good outcomes. It was considered that the use of RFID was only of merit during the research phase and that once there was a greater understanding of the process of returning cubs to the natal sett, its use was not critical other than for data collection. The success of recording a natal return hinged mostly on the RFID and its deployment too early after release could give a premature positive outcome result. A minimum period of two weeks should be sufficient in confirming that the cub was still in residence and a dual use of a trail camera would confirm its condition.

There is always the possibility that following release the cub could befall a natural accident which had no bearing on the fact that it had been released back at the sett. This is considered to be a natural occurrence and part and parcel of an animal living naturally in the wild. It has to be borne in mind that if a cub is not recorded at a sett following release there could be other factors influencing the outcome. Badgers have been observed to vacate a sett for weeks without any warning, only to return later.

FEEDING TUBE

This simple piece of equipment is useful in some situations especially for support feeding of badger cubs. It will encourage an animal to return to the same spot, which will then make the process of regular monitoring easier; see Fig. 1

I have used a feeding tube on various species (otter, fox. polecat) and found the best results are obtained when it is placed within the animal's enclosure prior to release. The animal is then fed normally within the tube to the point of release, by this time it will associate the tube with food. Utilising the actual tube on release is advised, as this will be 'scent familiar' to the animal.

A 1m section of plastic twin wall drainage pipe measuring 300mm dia. is the best configuration for badgers. It can have an access hole in the top (with a sliding cover) to allow the food to be placed easily into the tube. Cutting a section out of the pipe (lengthwise) prevents the pipe rolling around; see Fig. 1; inset picture. Tent pegs are useful in pinning the tube to the ground.

Fig. 1

Feeding Tube with RFID antenna fixed to the end. Top section slides sideways to reveal an opening in which food can be placed

CUB RELEASE CAGE (REMOTE OPENING)

This was a converted wire cat carry cage measuring approximately 400mm L x 300mm H x 300mm W. It was secured in place with the use of tent pegs to prevent the cage from moving or becoming dislodged. The top panel/door was hinged but during the release the cage was placed on its side so that the hinge was uppermost. Attached to the door was a counter weight that allowed the door to open outwards and upwards in a slow flowing movement (avoiding disturbing the cub or any other badger present). The door was held in a locked position by a metal pin which had a length of string attached to it. At the appropriate moment the pin could be pulled out and the door would rise gently, allowing the cub to move away; see Figs. 2-4.

The purpose of such a cage was to ensure continuity of a release. It was considered that there may be just one opportunity to release a cub at a sett, especially if this depended on a positive encounter with a sow.

Walking up to the cage and opening the door manually would break the connection between the cub and a sow.

CAMERA

Bushnell and Acorn trail (no-glow) cameras were used for general data collection. For live filming a general infra-red camera coupled with an Archos recorder/monitor was used. There was the option of a fixed wired camera and also wireless for some applications.

There are considerable issues associated with positively identifying a released animal when using a trail camera. How can you be sure the badger cub filmed at the sett is the actual one you released, or is it a sibling? Fur clipping is one option: see following section.

Fig. 2

Remote release cage (locked position)
Note: black pin with string (front
base left corner) and counter weight

Fig. 3

Pin withdrawn and door opening up
and outwards

Fig. 4

Door fully open

FUR CLIPPING

The technique of fur clipping badgers can be used to identify individual animals in the field, especially when used in conjunction with trail cameras; see Fig. 5. However this procedure is subject to a licence as this is considered as marking (see notes: Licence). Although I have only used this technique once on badgers, it did prove very effective when locating a single cub within a group of three others at a sett. It is important to clip responsibly and not impair the badger or cub with excessive clipping. A badger should not be fur clipped on the rump region, as this area is prone to fight related biting.

Fig. 5

Fur clipping, useful for identification but requires a licence

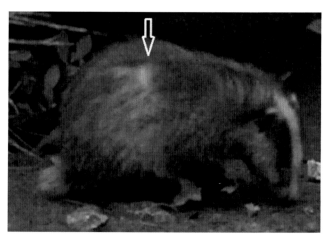

SUPPORT FEEDING EQUIPMENT

The process of implementing long term support feeding at some sites can be difficult and if there is no one to undertake a regular commitment then this may be a deciding factor in whether a release can be undertaken. In such cases the use of automated feeders could be considered. It is possible to buy automated pheasant feeders that will discharge peanuts see Fig. 6. This piece of equipment can be programmed to dispense peanuts in varying quantities at any given time; late evening would be most appropriate so that the food is not eaten by non-target species.

Another option for automated feeders is to build your own bespoke item. The benefits of this include low cost and making an item that is easy to conceal in an environment that may be subject to access by the public. Figs, 7-9 show an item that runs off a 12v/7ah battery and can dispense peanuts in varying quantities for up to 7days (depending upon the amount discharged and the hopper size). The unit discharges the peanuts via an auger (reclaimed from a hand mincer) and the electric motor is geared down, so that it dispenses in a more controlled manner than that of the pheasant feeder.

The main difference between the two is that the pheasant feeder is bulkier but will last longer between refills and it discharges the peanuts over a wide area. The model illustrated is fitted with a solar panel. The homemade unit is easier to camouflage and dispenses the peanuts over a small area. With the latter feeder, if the peanuts are allowed to drop onto a solid surface such as a concrete flagstone then the peanuts will bounce over a reasonable area preventing one animal dominating the food source.

During trialing of the pheasant feeder I wanted to be assured it was robust enough for field work. It was placed in a rehabilitation pen for 1 week with 7 large cubs and it survived unscathed. The same could not be said for the trail camera and tripod filming the feeder, which took the brunt of the cubs' inquisitive nature! It is not recommended that this feeder be utilised in areas where the public have access. The peanuts can ricochet off the spinning disc with a degree of force. This could be reduced by the fitting of a small screen around the unit to prevent the nuts from dispersing over a long distance.

It is recommended that dry dog food should not be used for support feeding cubs, especially if the weather is dry and water is not readily available at the sett. If dry food is used, then it should be thoroughly wetted and allowed to soak, adding more water if necessary. It is recommended that during dry weather support feeding should be accompanied by clean water in a container that is not easily soiled or knocked over.

Fig. 6

Automated feeder: 12v/7ah battery/solar charging. Peanuts drop on to a fast spinning disc and discharge them over a wide area. This type of feeder is better suited for feeding a whole group rather than a single cub.

Fig. 7

*Home made feeder: note discharge chute on RHS
of base*

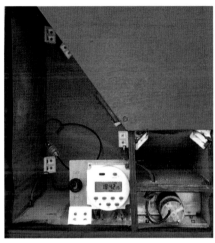

Fig. 8

*Door opened. Exposing timer and electric motor.
Battery not fitted*

Fig. 9

*Lid removed. Exposing safety guard and auger in
base of hopper*

CHAPTER 3:
CASE STUDIES: PRE-WEANED IMMOBILE CUBS UP TO 6 - 7 WEEKS

It would be impossible to provide examples of every type of rescue and release of a cub(s) to the natal sett. It is envisaged that the examples provided will give a broad range of incidents and age range of cubs. This will hopefully demonstrate how problems were overcome and a decision as to whether to attempt a release or refer the cub for LTR was made.

OPERATING PARAMETERS:

A cub of limited mobility would require a Monitored Natal Return (MNR) and would be vulnerable due to its age and lack of mobility. A cub would be micro-chipped (5-6 week) and monitored via remote IR camera; normally in the exact location they were found. Before proceeding, particular care is needed in assessing both the sow and cub's condition due to dependency on the sow. Minimal handling due to scent transfer, lack of food and heat loss during MNR must be considered. A positive outcome would be a lactating sow interacting with and picking up the cub and then removing it to a place of shelter, such as a sett.

This is followed up with RFID for assessment of long term outcome (for research purpose only).

DRAYCOTT

INTRODUCTION

In March 2011 the owner of a farmhouse (which had a number of dilapidated farm buildings) contacted SWWR to say they had found a small badger cub at the entrance to a sett within the curtilage of their farmyard. They were instructed to handle the cub as little as possible and they placed it in a box with some bedding and a warm bottle.

SITE SURVEY

I attended the site within two hours and found that the cub was approximately 5 weeks old with its eyes partially open; see Appendix 1 and Appendix 1A: Estimating the Age of Badger Cubs: Photographs, with all future references to cub ages. It appeared fit and healthy and quite active and importantly, vocal. The sett was located under a disused brick building and one entrance (where the cub was found) appeared to descend under the wall of the building with mounds of excavated earth and rubble outside on the ground. There was significant badger activity throughout the site and the landowner was very badger friendly. It appeared that the badgers were familiar and accepting of the owner and the family due to their close proximity and tolerance of the badger digging activity!

There was no report or evidence of any adult badger being injured or killed on the roads locally and on that basis I had an open mind as to the health and whereabouts of the sow.

As the cub was in good health it was felt that it would be worth holding the cub until the evening when the adults emerged and observing their behaviour towards the cub. It was reasonable to assume the cub had come from this sett complex, but unclear as to how it had ended up at the sett entrance. There was, however, some evidence of a recent clean out of the sett (spoil and bedding) and it is possible that the cub had become part of this 'debris'. Due to the size of the cub it was felt unlikely the cub had crawled upwards out of the sett.

During the examination of the cub surgical gloves were used to prevent any unwarranted scent transfer. The cub was kept warm (with a warm, hot water bottle) for the rest of the afternoon.

The landowners had good knowledge of the potential time the badgers would emerge, as they often came across the badgers within the farmyard.

ACTION

The evening was warm and the entrance sheltered from the elements so it was felt that the cub could be left in the open for a short period. The cub was placed at the sett entrance approximately 20 minutes before any adult badgers were likely to emerge. As the badgers were familiar with the landowner she was asked to place the cub down, so that my scent would not cause alarm. It was critical that my presence (scent) would not impede the emergence of the badgers from the sett.

The cub and sett entrance were monitored via a camera and a monitor placed in a disused car within the farmyard. The cub became very vocal and after about 15minutes an adult emerged from an entrance to the left (distance of 5m) of the one where the cub was placed, it ignored the cub and went off across the farmyard. The cub continued to give a "rapid-kecker" distress call (see glossary) and became more mobile and was crawling around the entrance. At this point it rolled down the entrance into the neck of the sett to a depth of about 1m. A quick decision had to be made as to whether to intervene or let nature take its course. There was a concern that the sow was either dead or had abandoned the cub and it had been ejected from the sett. I could not allow the cub to fall any further into the sett complex and out of reach. I considered this would be abandoning the animal at an age when it would not be capable of looking after itself. Despite concerns regarding my scent being placed on the sett entrance a decision was made to retrieve the cub and I quickly approached the sett and reached down into the tunnel and picked up the cub. The cub was placed back with a small log between the cub and the sett entrance to prevent a recurrence.

Unfortunately my scent was now on the cub (as in the haste to retrieve it, I had no time to find gloves) and my scent was also in the entrance of the sett and on the ground where I had laid whilst reaching down for the cub. Having studied badgers at length in the field I am acutely aware that the scent of a person unfamiliar to a badger can delay or even prevent a badger emerging from a sett. The cub continued to rapidly-kecker and within 5 minutes the camera picked up the eye reflection of an adult badger within the lower section of the sett entrance. It came further up the tunnel to the entrance where it moved its head around in a swaying motion from side to side presumably to get a better view and focus on what was happening with the cub. I also observed the adult flicking its head in the air, as they do when scenting the air for the presence of danger or to provide them with more information of their environment. After less than a minute at the entrance the adult moved closer to the cub, it reached over the log and carefully picked up the cub in its mouth and then returned quickly back down into the sett complex.

The cub had not been micro-chipped as it was of a small size and the smaller micro-chip was not available. There were concerns (mainly mine) that regular sized micro-chips were too invasive for a small cub without a good welfare reason.

The landowner was asked to monitor the sett following the return in case the cub reappeared but she reported nothing untoward over the next few weeks. Later in the early summer she did report seeing 4 cubs at the sett and it would not be unreasonable to assume one of these may have been that cub.

The fact that an adult badger overcame its fear or suspicion of my scent at the sett entrance is very important in this case and would lead me to surmise that this was the sow retrieving her cub. It can be impossible to state accurately the sex of a badger by appearance only, though on the whole boars can sometimes be identified by their broader head with sows having a narrower head, especially when looking at the width of the jaw around the hinge. It is by no means scientific, but this badger did fit the general features of a sow. Crucially I did not witness a large "boar type" animal engaging with the cub.

I have observed on many occasions an emerging adult badger scenting the air for long periods and retreating back into the sett when it has detected my scent on the ground from much earlier in the day (many hours prior). For an adult to emerge and pick up a cub with human scent only a few minutes old would indicate to me that there was a strong maternal bond between the cub and the badger that retrieved it.

This was my first natal return and a forerunner to the commencement of the full trial. Lessons were learnt, especially on the actual placement of the cub at the sett entrance and that despite its immature size it was still capable of movement into and down the sett entrance.

KEY POINTS

• Cub in good physical condition

• Very vocal, prompting a response from the sow

• The sow ignored my scent when retrieving the cub

• Relied heavily on knowledge from the landowner, especially associated with emergence times of the adults at the sett

• Cub initially too close to the entrance

SEWAGE WORKS

INTRODUCTION

In early March 2012 I was asked to attend a site where a firm of demolition contractors had removed a portakabin type structure that had been in-situ within a sewage works for many years. The contractors were using a 15 ton excavator to demolish the pre-fab building and then load it on to a series of 20 ton tipper wagons. Following the removal of all the outer structure and floor the machine operator began the task of grubbing up the concrete footings (on which the building had stood). These were large sections of concrete measuring approximately 350mm x 350mm x 2.5m in length. During this process the machine operator noticed movement in a pile of dry grass and leaves adjacent to the concrete slab he was attempting to pull out of the ground with the excavator. On close examination he realised there were three badger cubs within a pile of dried grass and twigs; see Fig. 10. Fortunately the contractors stopped work immediately and then contacted SWWR. Within an hour I was able to attend the site.

Fig. 10

"Nest" of grass, twigs and mosses containing 3 cubs

SITE SURVEY

The cubs were approximately 4-5 weeks old with their eyes still closed. All appeared to be in excellent condition with no visible injuries and despite being open to the elements they were warm and not stressed by their exposure.

There was no sett to speak of; just a scrape in the ground filled with dry mosses, leaves and twigs, the appearance of this structure could only be described as resembling a nest. A wider survey of the treatment works found various badger holes dug under brick structures. Two sett entrances (close to the cubs) were observed in the white limestone chippings at the base of a round sewage filtration bed. Contact with the Somerset Badger Group confirmed that badgers have been recorded at the site over a period of many years.

It was decided that the cubs should be inspected by a veterinary nurse (who had extensive experience with badgers) as there were concerns there may have been crush injuries in relation to the demolition and subsequent works. The cubs were kept in-situ within the nest and the veterinary nurse attended site and confirmed that the cubs were un-harmed. A decision was made not to micro-chip the cubs due to their size and to reduce the amount of handling involved. They were then covered with a high visibility jacket, firstly to protect them from being walked on and secondly to keep the wind from cooling them down; see Fig.11.

Fig. 11

High visibility jacket protects the cubs

The red line marks the precise position that the concrete footings (now stacked on the right of the photograph) were located. Note the position of the cubs (under the jacket) in relation to the line and the heavy demolition machinery on site.

It was thought that during the demolition of the building the sow had retreated across a small section of concrete path and under the perimeter of a filtration bed. This was approximately 15m from the cubs and the nearest hole/ sett accessible by the sow. No badger activity was evident to indicate that a sett may have been under the cabin and no paths or pass-under could be found to indicate that a sett was present.

ACTION

It was not clear if the sow would come back to the cubs, however I felt that it was reasonable to assume that if she was unharmed and provided with space and a quiet environment the sow might return. The contractors agreed to stop all further work for the day and left the site.

The high visibility jacket was removed and a warm but light blanket was then placed over the cubs. A cord was tied to one corner of the blanket so if an adult was observed in the vicinity, it could be removed remotely with little disturbance to facilitate quick contact between the sow and cubs.

I was able to park my car very close to the cubs and also have a good view of the sett entrance under the filter bed. This provided me with excellent cover and shelter as the night drew in. An infrared camera linked to a monitor was placed overlooking the cubs and I waited until it was dark.

At approximately 20:30 an adult badger was observed exiting the hole (nearest the cubs) from under the filter bed. At this point I slowly pulled on the cord and the blanket was removed from the cubs. It was observed (via the camera) that the cubs were still buried deep within their nest. The badger was extremely nervous and frequently scenting the air and pacing around. It repeatedly looked over to the area where the cubs were located; it then disappeared and returned about 45min later. It continued the same behaviour, pacing around the outer edge of the disturbed ground and it was very reluctant to venture onto the broken ground where the cabin had been located.

It is not clear if there had been some vocal stimulus from the sow (by this stage

I was convinced this was the sow to the cubs) but as she gained confidence and gradually got nearer the cubs it was observed that the cubs became active in the nest with one pushing through the grass, twigs and mosses into the open air. The sow was spurred on by this and eventually she walked onto the base and picked up one of the cubs in her mouth, holding it by the scruff of its neck; see Fig.12. Withdrawing quickly (cub keckering) she trotted off briskly, head aloft with the cub in her mouth and retreated back under the filter bed. The sow did not return and at 23:00 the remaining two cubs and nest were scooped up and placed at the entrance hole on the filter bed (where she had taken the single cub). Despite the remaining cubs' rapid- keckering, the sow did not return.

The temperature was now dropping and the cubs had been without food for some considerable time. At 23:50 it was decided, on welfare grounds, that the remaining cubs would be taken to SWWR. No further attempt to place the cubs back at the site was made as the cubs were very vulnerable and due to the ongoing site disturbance it was considered that the sow was unlikely to return. The remaining two cubs were admitted into a LTR programme.

FOLLOW UP

To highlight one of the issues associated with LTR is the necessity to blood test a cub 3 times for the presence of bTB. Unfortunately one of the cubs returned a positive result and was euthanised. Upon post mortem it was found to be free from TB on standard PM and culture.

KEY POINTS

• Cubs kept in-situ

• As little handling as possible

• Cubs assessed for condition and welfare

• Prior to the disturbance the sow had been looking after the cubs and they were in good condition

• Patience

• Remaining cubs taken into centre for welfare reasons

WHY DID THE SOW NOT RETURN FOR THE OTHER TWO CUBS?

There are a number of factors that may have had an influence on the sow not returning. From the moment the sow emerged from the hole under the filtration bed she was totally focused on the area where the cubs were located. There was obviously a bond between the sow and the cubs despite the scene of total destruction of the sett and the trauma she must have gone through as the building was demolished above. The cubs were silent throughout the period the sow was surveying the ground, only becoming "agitated" as she approached and this may have been due to cubs sensing her nearby, or some low level vocal stimulus. The sow was clearly traumatised by the events and I have never observed a badger so nervous and yet staying in a location. I believe that the sow did not view the cubs as individuals, but when she eventually gained the confidence to approach the cubs she just grabbed one and ran back to safety.

To compound the problem there was considerable background noise at the site with the filtration beds operating and a nearby floodlit skate board park contributing with random banging and shouting. The sow would have been reasonably tolerant of this disturbance, as these sounds are part of its home range, but with its heightened stress any random noise would potentially exacerbate what was already a difficult situation.

I believe that when the cubs did begin to rapid-kecker (when placed at the filter bed sett entrance) she was not able to hear them, or she had moved further afield via another exit on the other side of the filter bed. If the cubs had been slightly more advanced and the environmental conditions less prohibitive, then there may have been some merit in trying to return the cubs the following night. I am confident that if the sow had "discovered" the remaining cubs then she would have engaged and retrieved them.

Fig. 12

The sow reaches into the nest and removes a cub

COMMENT: DISTURBANCE OF A SETT

There are clear provisions for the protection of a badger and the sett under The Protection of Badger Act 1992. However, it has to be shown that any damage or interference was reckless or carried out with intent. I have investigated many situations where someone has deliberately or recklessly interfered with or destroyed a sett and subsequently assisted the police and CPS in these matters. I felt in this particular case; with limited field signs relating to the occupation of the underfloor space of the cabin, this was an unfortunate incident and would have been difficult to avoid without prior knowledge of the sett.

In reality this nest could have been constructed over a day or two as there were no excavations below ground level and merely a scrape on the surface filled with grass, twigs and mosses. The fact that the cubs were approximately 4 weeks old does not mean that they were born at this location. It is perfectly plausible that the sow moved the cubs to this location after they were born, this could have been a few days prior to the demolition. The Chairman (2012) of the badger group was able to reason with the site owners and they agreed to cover the cost of LTR of the two remaining cubs.

SOW/CUB BOND

The bond that a sow will have with her cubs even in the most distressing situations should not be underestimated; this is clearly demonstrated in the brief account: Wells as detailed below:

WELLS

In 2016 two 6 week old cubs were discovered when a small manure heap (probably containing a sett) was completely removed by a tractor-loader and nothing was left of the "sett". The heap was 4 months old. One cub was transported 5 miles on the back of a farm trailer containing the manure and dumped in a field only to be discovered by the contractor, who then reunited this cub with another cub found at the original site. When I attended site, a thorough inspection of the cubs revealed that miraculously they had escaped un-harmed.

It was reported that during the works an adult badger left slowly (un-hurried) from the rear of the manure heap (probably the sow). This was considered at the time to be a badger merely asleep on or near the manure heap and taking advantage of the heat generating from the manure.

The initial support for these cubs consisted of the cubs being reunited quickly; they were provided with warmth (dry hay) and then placed in a thick hedgerow at the rear of where the manure had been located. Privacy was essential (people were kept away from the cubs) allowing the sow an opportunity to return without being disturbed. The sow returned and retrieved her cubs in daylight, one 4.5hrs and the other at approximately 6.5hrs after the manure heap was removed. When the first cub was removed the remaining cub was placed in a small wicker basket. This provided protection from the weather and contained the cub in one place, as it was inclined to crawl around. The basket had no negative impact on the sow returning and retrieving her remaining 'abandoned' cub. The cubs had been handled and my scent was on the ground within the hedgerow but this did not appear to deter the sow from retrieving her cubs. The cubs were very vocal (which is always a good sign) and this may have had an influence in persuading the sow to return before night fall.

I felt very confident that the sow would return but I was surprised that this occurred during daylight hours. However, the location where the cubs were placed consisted of a thick hedge which was on the junction of two other hedges. These hedges had clear badger paths running through them and provided good connectivity with natural setts close by in the hedgerows.

Latrines were also noted within the hedgerow and these contained small stools. I have observed this feature previously when examining setts associated with just a sow and cubs. It is by no means scientific, but I have considered that latrines and small stools near an outlier sett may indicate the presence of a nursing sow. A reluctance on the part of the sow to forage widely from the natal sett during the early part of a cub's development, may result in reduced food intake, unless the sow is fortunate to have plentiful feeding opportunities nearby.

It is impossible to state with any certainty whether this manure heap actually contained a sett. It is possible that the sow had a couch or nest above ground, or a hollow on the back of the manure heap facing the hedge. Above ground nests or couches in hay are recorded; Neal and Cheeseman [6] detailing above ground nests and couches with daytime occupation. Couches/nests are not particularly rare and I do come across them occasionally. To find one occupied with cubs is possible, but I have never observed one in the field. As the whole structure of the manure heap had been removed by the time I attended site, we will never know the actual "sett" status of the manure heap. However I am satisfied that the landowner and contractor did not deliberately remove the manure knowing that there was a sett or badgers present. Their quick actions on discovering the cubs and the initial care advice from the badger group had a significant influence on these cubs surviving and being quickly reunited with the sow.

CHAPTER 4:
CASE STUDIES:
PRE-WEANED MOBILE CUBS

OPERATING PARAMETERS:

A cub becomes mobile (varying abilities) at approximately 6 weeks. By 8 weeks they will be exploring the tunnel system and the sett entrance. Issues associated with this group include: if placed near a sett or a hole the cub is likely to crawl or roll below ground without any known outcome. With mobile cubs, the cub is contained in a small cage where it is anticipated there will be interaction with the sow. The cage has a remote release mechanism and real-time camera monitoring. If a positive interaction is witnessed between cub and sow, the cage can be opened (remotely) and further observations witnessed. This is an MNR.

This is followed up with RFID for assessment of long term outcome (for research purpose only).

WORLE

INTRODUCTION

A badger was observed wandering along a busy local high street during the latter part of the afternoon in early January 2013. It was reported as a small cub, though this was thought unlikely because of the time of year and was probably a weak or injured adult. The rescuer who attended the site confirmed that it was a cub and it was then decided to bring it into SWWR for a closer examination. The rescuer was able to establish that two other cubs had been seen in the area at the time but they were more agile and had disappeared into the grounds of a small block of residential apartments.

The cub was examined by a vet and diagnosed as suffering from malnourishment; it was estimated to be approximately 10 weeks old and born in early to mid-October 2012. This season had been exceptionally wet in the south west with extensive flooding and constant rain had made most of the ground waterlogged, resulting in poor foraging opportunities.

SITE SURVEY

A site survey was arranged the following day with the rescuer, as they had firsthand knowledge of the location. The surrounding area was extensively developed consisting of mainly semi-detached 1920's or older residential properties, shops and a block of low rise apartments/flats. On examining the grounds associated with the residential flats (where the two cubs had last been seen) a worn pass-under was noted on a boundary concrete fence. Climbing up the embankment to the fence it was possible to see through a hedge (behind the fence) and observe a garden with clear signs of badger activity.

The homeowners of the garden were approached and they granted permission for us to undertake a survey. The garden was heavily planted with small trees and bushes and measured approximately 40m wide x 10m deep. At the rear of the garden there was a substantial boundary brick wall belonging to a commercial garage. There was an entrance to a sett adjacent to the wall that clearly went deep down and under the wall and probably beneath the concrete floor of the garage. All the field signs indicated extensive badger occupation including cub prints. To compound the problem for these cubs the weather had been atrocious and the garden was muddy and worn bare by frequent badger activity. A heavy canopy of trees blocked the little sunlight there was at this time of year; these cubs would have struggled to survive, especially through this winter period. There were also a number of holes indicating a sett complex under a shed within the garden, with potential undermining of this structure.

Surprisingly the homeowners had no idea that their garden was inhabited by badgers, though they had heard "noises at night". The realisation that they were sharing their garden with badgers was something they were not too happy to discover.

ACTION

It was clear that this cub and the other two observed had been born outside the normal cub rearing season (peak cub births occur in February). This in itself would have made the cubs survival very difficult as the availability of food is limited at this time of year. Adult badgers and their cubs born in or around February and raised through the summer will feed extensively in the autumn months boosted by an abundance of natural food. Extra fat reserves are built up and this helps badgers through the lean months of the winter. This is something these cubs will not have been able to do.

Although the homeowner was not 100% supportive of the badgers, they agreed that I could potentially return the cub. It was fortunate that an animal carer from SWWR lived close by and offered to attend the site (in their own time) every day to provide support food.

To help the homeowner I offered to ask an ecologist (who had extensive experience in badger related issues) to look at the badger sett and provide support and guidance on how to resolve their badger occupation. However, it was made clear that any substantial work could not be undertaken until the appropriate season (July-

November inclusive) due to legal requirements relating to the period when badgers can be extensively disturbed or a sett partially or fully closed down.

A trail camera was placed on the most active sett entrance near to the wall and over the next few days three cubs were observed at the sett, all larger than the one in the rescue centre. A sow was observed with clear feeding rings around her nipples; see Fig. 13. A larger badger was also observed which I concluded was probably a male.

After a week in rehabilitation it was agreed that the cub could be returned to the sett. There was compelling evidence that the sett was more than likely the one from which the cub had originated and that a sow, which had clearly given birth to cubs recently (outside the normal cub rearing season) was present. On that basis I did not undertake a full MNR. Instead the cub was taken to the garden in the late afternoon and placed within a cage away from the sett entrances. The cub immediately appeared to recognise its surroundings and frantically dug at the cage.

When the cage was opened the cub ran in the direction of the sett (wall) even though it could not see the sett at that point. This clearly indicated it recognised its surroundings and it disappeared down into the sett complex.

Fig. 13

Sow at sett

Support food was placed daily at the sett over the next few weeks during the initial monitoring period and then through the winter and into early spring. Trail cameras observed all four cubs and adults taking advantage of the food and the RFID confirmed the presence of the cub two weeks following its return; see Fig. 14

Fig 14

*Cub at sett following release,
note the wet ground*

KEY POINTS:

- Very unusual time of year for cubs of this size to be present

- It would have been easy to panic and keep this cub and the others in rehabilitation because of the time of year/lack of natural food and the poor weather

- Fortunate that a staff member of SWWR offered their time in extensive support feeding

- Without this supplementary food it was envisaged that all four cubs would have ultimately been admitted into the rescue centre

- Working with and supporting the homeowner

BABCARY

INTRODUCTION

In early May 2012 two cubs were found in a remote stable block when the landowner went to check their horses following heavy rain and extensive local flooding. The landowner was asked the size of the cubs; "bag of sugar", and their condition "no visible signs of injury and mobile". They also confirmed there was no adult badger present. The landowner was asked to close the stable door (no horse present) until someone could attend the site, this was to prevent the cubs from wandering off before the cubs and their situation could be assessed.

SITE SURVEY

The site and immediate paddock was located on a slight mound but the surrounding land was extensively flooded. I examined the cubs and both were in good condition; I estimated that their age was about 10-12 weeks old. The landowner was asked if he knew of any setts in the area and he indicated that there was a large sett about 500m away located on a hillside. I felt that it was unlikely these cubs would have vacated this sett as it would not have been directly affected by the flooding (but there was a possibility that it had become water logged). If, as suspected these cubs had been placed in the stable by a sow, I felt it was unlikely she would have taken the cubs from high ground down to low ground nearer the flooding.

There was a very small coppice about 25m from the stable but the landowner was not aware of any setts located within it: see Fig. 15.

I decided to investigate this area as it offered the nearest protection and cover close to the stable. Within the boundary of the coppice a number of flooded sett entrances were discovered adjacent to a stream. Around one of the entrances I observed badger paw prints in the mud, including adult and cub size prints. I felt reasonably sure that this was where the cubs had originated and the only reason they were in the stable was due to the adverse weather. It was reasoned that if the sow could be located and she was prepared to engage with the cubs then at this point there was no reason to take these cubs into a rescue centre.

Fig. 15

Coppice: view from stable of sparse coppice containing the sett

ACTION: ESTABLISHING PRESENCE OF THE SOW

A nesting box (700mm L x 450mm W x 400mm H; see Fig. 16) with bedding was placed in the stable along with puppy food, mashed up custard creams and water. The cubs were then micro-chipped. The stable was closed and a trail camera placed at the door to record any external activity. The door was closed to prevent the cubs from wandering off and looking for the sow and potentially falling into a flooded ditch or stream in the surrounding area.

On examining the camera the following morning it was noted that a sow was seen on a number of occasions through the night attempting to get to the cubs. The sow had clear evidence of having fed cubs recently, with highly visible feeding rings around her nipples; see Fig. 17. The cubs ate all the custard creams and some of the puppy food.

On the evidence observed I was able to conclude that the sow was alive and crucially she was trying to engage with her cubs. This was a lactating female and the probability of these being her cubs was very strong. On that basis an attempt to reunite the sow with the cubs would be undertaken in a controlled manner.

RE-UNITING THE SOW WITH HER CUBS

If the stable door was left open it was reasonable to assume that the cubs could wander off or allow access by other animals including farm dogs. A board was placed across the open stable door that was of a sufficient height to prevent the cubs from climbing out, but would allow the sow to climb over and attend to her cubs. It was envisaged that the sow would either remove the cubs at her own discretion or she would leave the cubs in the safety of the nesting box.

A camera was placed on the stable entrance to record any movement. The sow returned in the early evening and entered the stable a number of times; see Fig. 18-19. Later in the evening/early morning she removed the cubs individually by picking them up and carrying them over the board.

Fig. 18

Sow checks cubs

Fig. 19

Sow climbs over the board and retrieves her cubs

FOLLOW UP

Over the next few days the flood water on the surrounding land subsided allowing a more detailed survey of the immediate area to be undertaken. Unfortunately this did not reveal where the sow had taken the cubs. The flooded sett within the coppice was placed under surveillance via a trail camera and regular visits to the site were made. After two weeks fresh hay was placed at a sett entrance and within two days it had been taken into the sett.

Approximately four weeks following the cubs being reunited with the sow, both cubs were positively recorded at the sett via their micro-chip. The trail camera also recorded the cubs and sow feeding (on peanuts) at the sett; see Fig. 20.

Fig.20

Sow and cubs back at the natal sett

KEY POINTS:

• Cubs health was determined

• Reason for their presence was established

• Worked with landowner on the site

• Established sow was alive and engaging with cubs

• Provided sow access to the cubs and prevented them from wandering off

CHAPTER 5:
CASE STUDIES:
CUBS FULLY WEANED

OPERATING PARAMETERS:

Cubs found later in the season are more mobile and can potentially wander into a neighbouring territory, especially during periods of dry or adverse weather. In these cases the animal may need a period of rehydration/feeding/treatment within a rehabilitation centre and then be considered for release. During a release, older cubs are placed within a holding cage with a remote release facility. In such cases positive interaction with any badgers present, or if the animal becomes excited when the cage is placed near a sett or a badger path near a sett would be considered a positive outcome. Where an animal displays extreme caution or indifference to other badgers at the site or its environment then careful consideration must be given prior to any release, as this badger cub may be in the wrong territory.

This is followed up with RFID for assessment of long term outcome (for research purpose only).

FROME

INTRODUCTION

In June 2014 a badger cub was found above ground during daylight hours on a small sports field belonging to a primary school. The weather was dry and had been so for a number of weeks. The cub was taken into SWWR where it was assessed as approximately 16 weeks old and when examined by a vet it was found to be malnourished, and dehydrated. It was decided that an investigation of the grounds was worth undertaking to assess the situation and check that there were no other cubs in distress.

SITE SURVEY

The site was visited and the caretaker and head teacher were very supportive of wildlife and offered help. It was reported that there had been a dead adult badger seen on a side road some weeks earlier but on checking there was no evidence to confirm this report. A number of active setts were located on an embankment within the school grounds very close (25-40m) to the area where the cub was found. The presence of these setts was something that the caretaker and head teacher knew nothing about. It was reasonable to assume that the cub had surfaced during the day due to the adverse weather and it was probable that the cub originated from one of the setts on the site.

It was decided that a return would be attempted once the weather had improved and this would be supported with supplementary food and water. No other cubs were found, but the school was asked to keep a look out for any other cubs.

ACTION

The cub took a longer period of time to recover than initially envisaged and coupled with the extended dry weather the cub was not ready for release until it had been within the rehabilitation facilities for a period of 6 weeks. The site was re-surveyed for badger activity and this proved successful.

A decision to release the cub was made even though it had been in the facility for a considerable period. The deciding factors in this case included a good support package being available and the cub only being released if it indicated good site recognition. This recognition would be based upon placing the cub in a cage at the site and only allowing the release if the cub became excited with its environment. Upon release it would be observed and hopefully it would head directly to a known sett. Provision was in hand to recapture the cub (strong long handled net) if the cub wandered around the site in a random and unfamiliar manner. A fit badger cub can move through its environment very quickly and care was taken that the release was in open ground. It was envisaged that if there was a problem with the cub during release then there was sufficient open space in which to re-capture the cub, before it disappeared into difficult terrain.

Fig. 21

Cub in remote release cage, note partly covered to provide shelter

The cub was taken to the site in the early evening when the field was quiet. Once the cage (partly covered) was placed down on the grass the cub became very active and clawed at the cage; see Fig. 21. A decision to open the cage (via a remote cord) was made, upon which the cub exited the cage almost immediately. It wandered briefly around the cage (as though assessing its bearings) and then moved very positively to the shrubbery and hedge in which the major sett was located. I was able to witness the cub enter the top entrance of the sett and felt from the ground below me (I was on top of the sett at this point) a series of vibrations/bumps under the ground from badger activity.

A trail camera was positioned on a feeding tube within the hedgerow. The food and water was replenished every day for two weeks. The RFID was then installed at the feeding tube which coupled with the camera recorded the cub in good health. A further installation of the RFID at the sett (feeding tube) logged the cub 26 days following its release. Support food continued for a further 6 weeks on a diminishing basis until there was a sustained period of wet weather.

KEY POINTS

• Surveyed site for other cubs in distress

• Cub held in rescue facilities for 6 weeks before release

• Good support from landowners

• Cub showed clear site recognition when released and did not wander around as though in unfamiliar surroundings

• A strong net was to hand if the cub required re-catching

WEST HUNTSPILL

INTRODUCTION

In June 2013 a family returned from holiday to find a badger cub trapped within their garden. It was not clear how it became trapped as the garden had high fences around to keep their dogs enclosed and prevent badgers from getting in! The cub was taken into SWWR for assessment by the veterinary care team and was found to be approximately 12-14 weeks old and dehydrated but otherwise in reasonable condition. The weather at the time was dry and had been so for a number of weeks.

SITE SURVEY

The site was surveyed and a large sett was located directly next to the house within some overgrown derelict land. The sett was impossible to fully survey as it was extensive and screened with very tall and vigorous nettles, brambles and shrubbery. The homeowner agreed to put out food (supplied by SWWR) and water daily, if an attempt to release was made.

ACTION

Following a period of 14 days within the centre the cub was taken to the site in the late afternoon. The cage was placed within a bare patch of the nettles that contained a labyrinth of badger paths. As soon as the cage was placed down on the ground the cub became frantic and rapidly-keckered and clawed at the sides of the cage. The cage was opened up and the cub bolted along a badger path and directly into the sett complex. I was left with no doubt that the cub recognised this location.

Support food was provided for approximately 4 weeks by the homeowner until the weather improved and then reduced on a diminishing basis. The RFID and a trail camera were placed on an active sett entrance 10 days after the release. It was a further 5 days before the cub was detected on the RFID. This was thought to be as a result of the extensive nature of the sett and my suspicions that this sett may have been partly vacated by the badgers for a short period.

KEY POINTS

• Typical example of a cub trapped due to exploring its environment

• Cub exhibited good sett recognition

• Persistence was required in obtaining the RFID results as it became apparent this sett was vacated by the badgers for a short while, returning after about 7 days

ROWBERROW

INTRODUCTION

In May 2011 two 14 week old cubs were found in an old stable/railway goods wagon by a landowner attending to their horse. The weather had been dry for a number of weeks and both cubs appearing to be a little dehydrated. On closer examination at SWWR (by the veterinary care team) it was revealed that one cub (later named Kevin; see Fig. 22) had a fractured front leg. This was thought to have occurred as a result of it following a horse in the field and the subsequent displeasure from the horse over the cub's attention. The behaviour of a badger cub following a large animal such as a horse (or person) is not unusual and may indicate a cub being separated from the sow whilst malnourished.

Kevin would require a long period of rehabilitation and could not be considered for an early return. His sibling, another male, was suitable for a potential release subject to a successful survey.

Fig. 22

Kevin in a plaster cast, he required LTR but his sibling was released early

SITE SURVEY

The landowner was approached and they indicated that there were a number of setts on a heavily wooded steep embankment adjoining their field. A survey revealed a number of large setts in various states of activity at the uppermost section of the wood which adjoined a neighbour's field. It was concluded that the cubs had possibly migrated down the steep embankment (a distance of approx.100m) and became lost, taking shelter in the stable at the bottom of the embankment. It was noted that most of the badger paths radiated in either direction along the top of the embankment or out at the uppermost section of the wood boundary and across the adjoining fields. I was unable to locate any significant badger paths leading from the sett down the embankment to the field where the cubs were found. This may explain why the cubs did not find their way back up to the sett, as there were fewer paths and scent trails to navigate a return.

ACTION

It was highly probable that the cubs had originated from this sett complex but this was not 100% certain. It was decided if a release was to take place it would have to be on the grounds that the cub displayed good site recognition and preferably with a positive reaction from an adult badger. Although the cub was at a stage where it could find its own food, it would be irresponsible to release it in the wrong territory.

The cub was taken to the sett in the early evening two days after it had been brought into the centre. It was difficult to make a decision as to which cluster of setts to attempt a release and then which entrance to target. This was narrowed down to a sett that was particularly active and showed signs of the vegetation having been flattened, possibly by cubs playing. This sett also had one entrance with fresh bedding material deposited outside, which may have indicated the presence of a nursing sow, but at the very least recent activity.

The cub was placed down in a remote release cage in the early evening 6m from an entrance and observed from a safe distance of approx. 12m. A large ash tree served as a good support on which to lean and conceal my presence with the added benefit of it being down wind of the sett. The eyesight of a badger is not very acute but they rely heavily on silhouettes especially in a familiar environment. The ash tree provided an ideal natural screen. I soon realised that I had arrived too early at the sett and whilst the cub showed signs of sett recognition and rapidly keckered for approximately 20-30 minutes it eventually became tired and fell asleep. The cub had to be awakened on a number of occasions in anticipation of the emergence of any badgers. This was something I wanted to avoid as it placed the release in jeopardy. By approaching the cub I ran the risk of disturbing an emerging badger and in the process I was laying down my scent on the ground in the area of the sett.

As dusk approached, an adult badger emerged from the nearest entrance (bedding entrance) to the cub and despite the cub being awake and active in the cage it completely ignored the cub and set off through the wood. The cub continued to rapidly kecker and shortly a slimmer adult badger emerged at the sett complex higher up the slope approximately 10-15m from the cub. The reaction of this badger was completely different and it approached the cub in the cage and then proceeded to walk briskly around the cub in a large circle. It was so intent and fixed on the cub that at one point it actually stood on my foot without realising I was present. The cub remained vocal and was clawing at the cage; the adult badger approached the cage and walked around it cautiously and engaged in nose to nose contact. I decided to open the cage (remotely) unfortunately this disturbed the adult badger which moved quickly back in the direction of the sett, but stopped midway and turned around to view the cub again. The cub ran up the embankment (away from the nearest entrance with the bedding) and joined the badger. Both the cub and adult badger then ran back together into a well-used entrance within a larger sett complex.

At this juncture in time the RFID system was not available as it was broken, though the cub had been micro-chipped. When I was eventually able to undertake a follow up at the site it was spring the following year. There had been a dramatic change at the site and all the setts appeared to be disused or with very low levels of activity.

The RFID was utilised in a number of locations but no chip was recorded. Importantly the trail camera also failed to record any badger activity despite being in-situ for two weeks. I could only conclude that this location had been abandoned in favour of another site or something untoward had happened to the whole of this social group.

I would consider this release to be a success as all the signs and reactions of both the cub and adult badger gave strong signals of this cub being at the right sett and within its own social group. What happens after a release especially some 9-10 months later is out of our control. What is important is that the needs of each badger cub is taken into account; Kevin was admitted for a long period of rehabilitation and was then successfully released with a group of other cubs in September that year. The cub that was able to be returned was done so safely and in a controlled manner.

KEY POINTS

• Good example of assessing the needs of each cub and an appropriate response; one staying within the rehabilitation facilities due to its fractured leg and the other returned back to the natal sett

• Good sett recognition by the cub

• Positive reaction by an adult badger at the sett

CHAPTER 6:
CASE STUDIES: SUPPORT FEEDING

OPERATING PARAMETERS:

Weaned cubs that are found near to the sett but are struggling due to adverse weather conditions e.g. drought, or the recent loss of a post-lactating sow, can be assisted with support food. The emergence of cubs in daylight is often a good indicator that the cubs are struggling. Support food and water can be provided at the sett and then monitoring via a trail camera can ensure the uptake of food and identify any underlying health issues of the cubs monitored. In these cases a method that has been used successfully is the utilisation of a feeding tube see Fig. 1. The tube is secured to the ground to prevent movement and the food placed within the tube. The main issue with placing uncovered food at the sett is competition from other species such as foxes and corvids. It has been observed that unless foxes/corvids have previously been fed in feeding tubes (rescue centre) then they are generally wary of new objects.

Alternatively food can be placed under 450mm x 450mm ply boards see Fig. 26. Ideally, support food would be partially covered and as the badgers become familiar with the feed location, the food can then be completely covered with a board. If support feeding is undertaken over a period of more than a week then care should be observed in gradually reducing the food and not simply stopping. If the food is being targeted early by non-target species then once the badgers are familiar with the boards they can be weighted down with a stone or half brick. The badgers will easily remove these objects but other species are less inclined or lack the strength to do so. Avoid using dry food especially in periods of hot weather.

Occasionally a report will come in that a dead lactating sow has been found near to a sett. In this case any cubs pre-weaned will be dependent on the sow for milk and if the cubs can be located and caught they will have to be admitted to a rescue centre for LTR. However what should be done if a dead sow is found that is considered to be post lactating and the cub(s) can be located but they are not dependent on the sow for milk? Every rescue situation is different and there will be local knowledge that may affect a decision. Generally cubs that are weaned and established as part of a social group can be support fed and not brought into a centre for LTR.

TAUNTON (1)

(Initial site survey and monitoring by Vanessa Mason; Somerset Badger Group)

INTRODUCTION

In May 2014 a member of the public reported a cub sitting on a dead adult badger on a quiet country lane; this was investigated by a member of the local badger group. The badger was a lactating sow, but it was evident (by extensive feeding rings) that any cubs reliant on the sow would potentially be of a large size and either weaned or nearly weaned. The longer a sow feeds her cubs the more pronounced the feeding rings will become and in some cases the whole underside around the nipples becomes bare and devoid of hair. There was no sign of the cub when the site was initially visited.

Irrespective of the report of this cub, a dead badger involved in a RTC within the cub rearing season (Jan-June) should always be investigated (providing it is safe to do so) to establish if it is a nursing sow.

SITE SURVEY

A site survey by the badger group revealed a good sized sett within a nearby coppice adjacent to a quiet minor B-road and another sett within an embankment/ hedge on the other side of the road. A camera was installed at the coppice sett which revealed at least one cub that was approximately 12-14 weeks old.

ACTION

It was decided that a course of support feeding would be undertaken as the cub was of a reasonable size (weaned) and there was no compelling reason to try to attempt capture it at that time. It would also have been problematic to try and install a cage trap due to the public having access to the site and the presence of other badgers. A trail camera was installed to monitor the uptake of the food. The weather had been dry for a few weeks and the cub made good use of the water and food placed at the sett. It became apparent that when the images were inspected there were two cubs in need of assistance.

On the evening I attended the site a cub was noticed at one of the sett entrances associated with the embankment/hedge sett. It returned into the sett as I approached. Wet dog food and peanuts were placed in the sett entrance. Food would not normally be placed in the entrance to a sett but I wanted the cub to have access to the food quickly and potentially gain immediate information on its condition. I retreated to my vehicle and then re-checked the entrance a few minutes later. The cub had re-emerged and was eating the food; see Fig. 23. Sufficient food to support more than one badger was placed at the sett. This is important as it cannot always be guaranteed that the cub(s) in need will emerge first and find the food.

A local supporter of the badger group continued to place food at this sett and the other sett across the road over a period of many weeks until the weather improved (damper conditions) and then the support food was reduced gradually.

It is not possible to state with any certainty if the cub survived long term (end of autumn), but I reasoned the course of action was the most appropriate as it was not considered dependent on the sow for food. It was not clear how much support a sow would provide after lactation has finished. My own observations of cubs and a sow in the field indicate that the cubs do forage with the sow and at other times she will leave the cubs unattended. Obviously the lack of a sow may put a cub at some disadvantage. However the loss of a sow (with cubs) is a frequent occurrence within the natural world and I felt that the support food taken by the cubs could make all the difference to their survival especially during inclement weather

Fig. 23

Cub quickly appeared and took advantage of the support food

KEY POINTS

- Support feeding in adverse weather conditions can be very effective, providing consistent and reliable help is available locally

- The volunteer who provided the food regularly also supported other cubs (different social group) in a nearby wood that had been seen searching for food during daylight hours

- Consideration is needed to allow extra food where more than the 'target badger' is located

- Food was placed in a number of food stations on the site to prevent one animal dominating the food source

- The presence of the road and potential risk to the badgers is of concern, but we have to respect that this sett was well established with good sett occupancy. It would not be right to remove a reasonably mature cub from this location based on the road "issue" alone

ESSEX

(Account and sett monitoring by Derek Barry) abridged by A. Parr

INTRODUCTION

I had a call out for an RTA of a dead badger on the 19th April 2013 in the Uttlesford area. When attending an RTA of a badger, especially during the breeding season, consideration must be given to the possibility of a suckling sow. In this case it became apparent that the badger was a lactating sow, though the only difference was the sow had limited milk and it was assumed that the cubs would be nearly weaned. I now had to establish where did she come from and how would the cubs cope without their mother?

On occasions when a sow is killed at the side of a road and it is fully lactating, milk can sometimes "leak" onto the road or be expressed, even after death. It was considered that any cubs attributed to this sow would be weaned or nearly weaned. This however should be used as a guide only. A sow may be deficient in milk before weaning is complete especially if she is experiencing problems in feeding due to sickness or general lack of food within its territory: A. Parr.

SURVEY

I noticed a man across a field in his garden. I needed some local knowledge and perhaps he would know where there were badger setts close to hand. I shouted across to him and he came over. I explained what had happened to this badger; he said he had seen it earlier but did not know what to do about it. I informed him that I needed to find this badger's sett as quickly as possible. I pointed out the light coloured mud on the badger's fur and he said that there was an area with the same light coloured soil, in the field opposite where he lives and that there were a number of holes along the edge of the field.

I made my way round the headland of the field towards them. I came upon a number of holes that the farmer had gone around during ploughing and determined that this was a badger sett. As I looked down one of the larger, deep tunnel entrances, there at the bottom, were three badger cubs. I laid on the ground and eased my way closer to the entrance to get a better view; they looked to be at least two months old and were in good shape; see Fig. 24 and Fig. 25 (sett later in the year). They were moving around the tunnel, occasionally growling at each other and biting the nodules of hard soil at the base of the tunnel.

ACTION

I was faced with a dilemma, are these the dead sow's cubs; I assumed that they were and on that basis what steps should be taken in dealing with them? I gave Andy Parr a call whilst I still had the cubs in view. We both agreed that the best approach (at this stage) would be to provide some puppy food with plenty of meat jelly/gravy, placing it within the sett entrance. The gravy along with the moist tinned meat would help substitute for the lack of fluids.

The next step was to find the farmer who owned this field and get his permission to allow local volunteers to go on his land to put food down for these cubs on a regular basis. I was able to locate the farm manager and he informed me that he knew about the dead badger having seen it earlier; it was first seen at 05.30 am that morning. I asked the manager if there were any other setts close to where the dead badger was found and he said the one associated with these cubs, was the nearest. I was given permission to support feed the cubs, though it did require some tactful negotiations.

A decision to support feed was then agreed and this would allow the true status of these cubs to be established. If it was found that these cubs were orphaned and not coping well (even with the support food) we would be in better position to capture them and bring them into a centre for LTR, especially if they were habituated in taking food at the sett.

Fig. 24

Cub as first seen on the day of the survey

Fig. 25

The multi-holed sett later in the season

(The age of these cubs would be at the lower scale of when weaning begins and the fact that the sow appeared to have little milk may have indicated a lack of sustenance or a sow not necessarily in the peak of fitness; A. Parr)

I asked a volunteer to keep an eye along a deep ditch near to the sett for any of the cubs that might have ventured out during the night and tumbled down into the ditch. I also asked a volunteer to warn her neighbour to keep their small dog away from the sett, particularly as the smell of dog food will drift up from the sett and might attract the dog to venture below ground.

To help find out if there were any adult badgers present at this sett, I monitored it every night over a period of a week using IR trail cameras. Unfortunately, no adults were seen and none of the peanuts put out for them on the surface were eaten, though a lone fox ate some. The three cubs however had eaten the chicken in gravy / jelly placed into the tunnel by Teresa and Mark (local volunteers). Their input into the support feeding was essential and they provided food twice a day.

Of the three cubs, two of them clung to each other; the third cub remained in the background, we call this one Solo. The cubs cleared up the food as soon as they surfaced in the evening. It was observed that Solo was regularly pounced upon by the dominant cub and Solo tended to stay close to the entrance tunnel and we were worried that it was missing out on the food. It was decided to divide the food amongst the other entrance tunnels during the day feed, but during late evening, spread the food further away from the actual sett entrances.

During this early period, one of the cubs had taken a fancy to what I thought was eating the leaves of the Rape Seed Oil crop in that field. On closer examination of the camera recordings it became apparent that the cub was not eating the leaves but licking the moisture from them. It was considered that the tins of dog food were not providing sufficient fluids. Water was then provided and this was regularly used by the cubs, especially during later periods when the nearby ditch had dried up: see Fig. 26.

After a week of daily monitoring at the sett with the IR trail cameras, it was established that these cubs were indeed orphaned and entirely on their own. It appears that they would not have had the opportunity to bond with many adult badgers, excluding the sow. Andy and I pondered over this point and concluded these cubs are in a similar situation as those that are taken into a rescue centre and put into a family group of other orphaned cubs. However these cubs are in a natural sett where they were born and they would have the advantage of learning life skills much earlier than those from a LTR environment whilst being support fed.

These cubs were too young to be able to dig and forage for food proficiently, but it was observed they instinctively went through the motions of digging for grubs and one cub in particular dug out some soil from the sett entrance. When bedding of hay was placed outside the sett entrance, it was pulled into the tunnel by the dominant cub: see Fig 26.

Fig. 26

Note: Hay supplied for bedding, water bowl and food covered with ply

Three months following the intervention, I continued to monitor the cubs with three IR cameras and additional IR Illuminators. The latter was carried out over alternating evenings for a number of weeks. Over a phased period the feeding stations were moved further away from the sett to encourage exploration of their local environment.

By the autumn the support food was reduced as the sightings of the cubs became less frequent. As the cubs matured it became increasingly difficult to differentiate whether the cubs recorded were the original badgers or other local badgers from the same or an adjoining social group.

Support food was generously provided by: Animal Rescue Charity in Bishop's Stortford

KEY POINTS

- Report of a dead badger was investigated quickly

- Excellent environmental observations in matching the mud on the sow with the sett

- Local knowledge was crucial in locating the sow with the sett

- A thorough survey resulted in locating the cubs quickly

- Local people were engaged and undertook support feeding

- Cameras were essential in providing an up to date condition of the cubs and their welfare. This resulted in water being provided and the food being spacing out to prevent dominance by one cub over the food source

- Care was taken to ensure the cubs did not become imprinted to the people providing the support food

COMMENT

(By A. Parr)

I would consider that the presence of the three cubs into the autumn would indicate this process was a success. Mortality rates for cubs in the wild are high, even with a sow present. The support food and monitoring was essential in ensuring these cubs did not enter LTR, but gave them the very best possible chance in the wild and within their territory.

The lack of an adult badger at the sett was obviously not ideal. However, it was considered that these cubs were of sufficient maturity (just) to be able to cope reasonably well in this sett complex and if supported with food, then they should not be admitted immediately into LTR (that's assuming they could be caught). It must also be noted that this sett and cubs were being extensively monitored and if the situation deteriorated, then provision was in place to try and capture these cubs. It should be remembered that cubs will learn essential life skills every day they are living in the wild. This is something they would not learn if admitted into a rehabilitation centre. A typical cub entering LTR will spend 6 or 7 months living in an environment that will not necessarily challenge or hone its survival skills. When a cub is released following LTR it will experience a very steep learning curve associated with survival in the wild. Not all badger cubs associated with this type of release will survive.

CHAPTER 7:
CASE STUDIES:
RELEASES NOT SUCCESSFUL

OPERATING PARAMETERS:

Of the cubs that I have personally taken for natal return, approximately 50% are not released and they are returned to the rehabilitation centre and become part of a LTR group. This is because conditions or cub behaviour provided me with sufficient concerns to halt the process. 'Failures' are as important as successful returns because we can learn from the cub's behaviour at a release site. Those that do not exhibit good recognition of their environment may in all probability be in the wrong territory or their actions may be masking underlying health issues.

ROCHDALE

(Account and release by Jo Bates-Keegan; Lancashire Badger Group)

INTRODUCTION

Towards the end of May 2012 during an extremely dry spell of weather, we were called out to a cub (approximately 12 weeks old, weaned) that had been in a domestic garden for a period of approximately 4 days. On our attendance at the property, the cub was found curled in direct sunlight within only a few feet of the family who were sitting on their patio.

The cub was immediately collected and provided with water and a little food. Later the cub was seen by a vet. The badger cub was assessed as being dehydrated and was kept in a garage (with natural light) for approximately 3 days in order to recover.

SITE SURVEY

A sett was identified approximately 100m to the east of the garden, which appeared to be an outlier showing signs of residence by badgers. Cub prints were noted. There was also a badger path along the edge of the garden, along which the owners of the property frequently saw badgers pass and enter the garden for food which was left out for them. A main sett was found approximately 250m to the south west of the garden

ACTION

It was decided that the badger cub should be released after 3 days, having shown strong signs of recovery. The cub was returned to the garden from which it was collected at approximately half an hour before sunset. The cage was placed in the garden within

23m of the badger path and the handlers withdrew. The cage door was connected to a piece of strong string to allow remote release of the door. It was our intention to watch the reaction of the cub and any other badgers in the vicinity. There were concerns that the behaviour of the cub prior to being picked up was unusual, especially if it was so close to a badger path it knew already. The cub did not appear to react to its surroundings. One local badger began to approach the cage but withdrew and the cub showed no reaction. Once the local badger had moved on, it was decided that the cage should be opened. The cub was gently encouraged to leave the cage but was reluctant to do so and instead it approached the handlers in an aggressive manner. At this point it was obvious that the cub was not in an environment it recognised and it was re¬collected and taken back to the rehabilitation facility.

After further consultation it was decided to attempt a release the following night nearer to the main sett, with the facility to remotely open the cage should the badger cub show signs of recognition. The cage was placed approximately 30m from the main sett on a well-used badger path approximately 45 minutes before sunset. The cub again showed no behaviour suggesting it recognised its surroundings and remained curled up and asleep. At one point it did briefly wake up and look around but a lack of real interest and determination to escape the cage caused enough concern to the handlers that the cub was not released. At no point did the cub appear to know where it was or attempt to leave the cage. After 45 minutes the release was abandoned and the cub was admitted to a rehabilitation centre for LTR.

It is considered that the cub had become separated from the sow and had found itself in the wrong territory, or had been the offspring of a subordinate sow and had been kept away from the rest of the clan. However, the former explanation seems most likely given its proximity to an outlier sett from which it could have readily returned.

KEY POINTS

• Cub treated and then assessed fit for release

• The reactions of the cub to its environment were closely monitored

• The cub showed no recognition of its environment so was admitted for LTR

TAUNTON (2)

INTRODUCTION

A 12 week (approx.) old cub was found wandering in the grounds of a school during daylight hours, the weather had been relatively dry and the cub was taken into SWWR for an examination by the veterinary care team. It was found to have minor dehydration and following three days of treatment it was considered suitable for release.

SITE SURVEY

On surveying the immediate area where the cub was found, a single entrance sett was located with signs of recent use. The landowners were supportive and stated that if the release was successful they would be prepared to support feed and provide water daily. It was decided to take the cub along in the evening in a remote release cage and wait for the potential emergence of the sow or other badgers.

The cub was placed in the cage about 5m from the sett entrance and the cub and entrance were observed from a safe distance. This was initially by direct observation but as darkness fell I utilised an infrared camera. The cub did exhibit some signs of excited behaviour at the site but it soon became quiet and remained calm especially during the latter part of the evening. The sett entrance was observed from 19:30 to 23:15 and no badgers emerged. A decision to terminate the release was made with a general feeling that it was unlikely any badgers were in residence (that evening). As the weather was dry, I felt that if any badgers were in the sett they would emerge early (as observed in other districts at the time) because of poor foraging opportunities and the pressing need to find water and sustenance. It is considered that this sett was an outlier and the location of the main sett is unclear.

KEY POINTS

The cub was taken back to the rescue centre and the following day it was decided that no further release would be attempted. This decision was based on the following reasons:

• The site did not have a level of activity that would indicate frequent badger use

• There were no significant signs of cub(s) having been active (in- play) on the surrounding rough vegetation

• Access difficulties with the site for long night-time observation

DEVON

INTRODUCTION

In 2014 a cub was brought into SWWR after it was found wandering at the edge of a very busy B-road/garden in Devon. It was in reasonable condition but a little underweight and was approximately 14 weeks old.

Despite the long distance from the rescue centre a decision was made to survey the site.

SITE SURVEY

The weather during this period was dry and the opportunities for badgers to forage for invertebrates would have been limited, except for more mature/experienced animals.

The landowners were very accommodating (former farmers who had retired to a bungalow and some 5 acres of land) and allowed me to survey their land and showed me the sett that was nearest to where the cub was found. There was one sett consisting of two holes within a grass roadside embankment that looked reasonably active, but its entrances were only 1m from the edge of the road. There was no verge and therefore I could not consider attempting to release a cub literally on the roadside. A single entrance sett was located on a scrubby embankment approximately 20m from the road. There was also another sett some 30m from the road within a flat section of a field. It was considered that a potential release be undertaken at the latter two setts (at least to check for familiarity).

The reasoning for considering a release at a sett close to the road was based on my experience that badgers do have setts near busy roads and this has to be respected. However I would not be prepared to release a cub actually on a roadside, because of the danger to the animal and potentially from the uncertainty of where the cub might go and the risk of an accident.

ACTION

Two days later the cub was taken to the site in the early evening. It was a long journey, so on arrival the cub was allowed to acclimatise to the surroundings before the cage was placed on the ground.

At the first sett within the field, the cub remained calm and disinterested in the location. The cage was left for 5 minutes before I then moved it slightly onto another badger path radiating from the sett. Again the cub appeared disinterested. The cage was then moved near to the sett on the embankment, but again the cub was subdued. The cage was then moved onto a path leading from the entrance but this had no effect on the behaviour of the cub; in fact it curled up and went to sleep. As the cub was not interested in its surroundings and did not appear to recognise the environment or pick up any familiar scent of its social group, a decision was made to take the cub back to the centre and it was entered into a LTR programme.

The landowner stated that there were other setts near-by (600m) but it was felt that this cub may possibly have come into another group's territory and there was not enough confidence in releasing the cub in this location. To compound the problem the weather had been very dry and establishing setts that were occupied with very poor field signs was almost impossible, especially when our base was located such a distance from where the cub was found.

KEY POINTS

• Although the sett at the roadside was showing signs of recent occupation I had concerns over the cub's welfare and general health & safety (traffic) if a release was attempted directly next to a busy road

• The cub displayed little recognition of its surrounding environment

• Dry weather made surveying difficult

• The distance from the rehabilitation facility to the site was a deciding factor as the level of surveying and monitoring required was considered prohibitive

CHAPTER 8:
RESULTS

RESEARCH RESULTS

It is clear that the return of badger cubs following short periods of rehabilitation can be very successful across all spectrums of the age range. Each age range requires a different approach and an understanding of the issues relating to the cub's physical condition and environmental conditions prevailing at the time. Once these have been established it is then possible to make a decision as to whether a cub is suitable for a return to the natal sett or not.

DURATION IN REHABILITATION/RELEASE

Important: This is based on the assumption that the cub has been assessed by a vet or suitably qualified person and considered suitable for release.

PRE-WEANED IMMOBILE OR LIMITED MOBILITY

Where there is a cub that is pre-weaned and up to approximately 8 weeks old, then there is a pressing need to return such a cub as quickly as possible. Although the timeline has not been fully explored I would suggest that a cub below 2 weeks old should be returned immediately. Cubs above this age range 2-5 weeks old, then this should be undertaken within 1-3 days. A cub up to 7-8 weeks old will probably not have naturally explored its environment beyond the sett entrance or very immediate sett area and you will be relying mainly on the sow/cub interaction at the sett.

PRE-WEANED MOBILE

Cubs in the age range of 8-12 weeks will have a stronger bond with the sow and its immediate (sett) surroundings. On that basis these cubs can potentially spend up to two weeks in rehabilitation. If they are in the younger age range then up to 1 week in rehabilitation is acceptable extending up to 2 weeks as they reach the upper age. As a cub explores its wider environment (beyond the sett) they will be capable of significant site recognition.

FULLY WEANED

It was established that a cub can be within a rehabilitation facility for some considerable time and still accepted back into its social group. In the case of Frome, the cub spent 6 weeks in rehabilitation and was subsequently logged 26 days following its release. Whilst this time period may be exceptional it should be noted that this was a fully weaned cub, familiar with its territory. Cubs in the age range of 10-12 weeks old were returned following up to 2 weeks in rehabilitation.

The cubs in this age range benefited significantly from support feeding especially during periods of dry weather.

GENERAL RESULTS

BEHAVIOUR

Significant differences in behaviour were observed with cubs and adult badgers over the course of the research. Some cubs showed distinct excitable behaviour when at a sett and others remained subdued and almost indifferent to their surroundings. Cubs that exhibited a significant level of excitement at the sett were generally released and this was followed by clear indications that they had been released in familiar territory. This could be observed by their ability to select an individual sett entrance to enter (sometimes not the nearest) or where the sett entrance was not obvious, the cub would automatically know where to go.

What did become clear is that those cubs taken to locations where there were low levels of badger activity or there were concerns that the cub may have travelled some distance (over 300m), these animals were rarely released as the level of activity and potential sett/scent recognition by the cub appeared to be low.

Interaction between a cub and sow (pre-weaned) proved to be very interesting in a number of ways. A sow that was keen to engage with her cub(s) would overcome considerable constraints such as stress and trauma (Sewage Works) or unfamiliar human scent on the cub and within the sett entrance (Draycott). The adult badger at Rowberrow became so fixated on the (weaned) cub in the release cage, that it actually walked on my foot and failed to respond to my scent, so strong was its focus on the rapidly keckering cub.

Observations were made of badgers from the same social group that completely ignored a cub and wandered off foraging. Although the sex of these badgers cannot be accurately determined, those observed did fit the generalisation of a boar. What is clear is that not all badgers in a social group will engage with a cub at the sett (when in a cage) and it is often a badger that fits the stereotype of a sow, which will engage. This is an important detail as it does allow a level of some control over the release. If there was a situation where all badgers within a social group readily engaged with the cub, then in the case of a cub that is not weaned it would be harder to establish if the sow was present and prepared to engage with the cub. It should also be noted that when cubs are young, trying to identify a lactating sow can be difficult as clear signs of feeding rings are not always visible. Therefore the fewer adult badgers showing an interest in a cub would make the identification of the sow potentially easier.

It could be argued that the reason a cub failed to recognise its surroundings was due to general ill health or underlying health issues, as opposed to being in the wrong territory. This does have to be considered, but I was not aware of any of the cubs I brought back into the centre (as a failed return) subsequently suffering from significant ill health. I would suggest that the reason so few failed returns went on to exhibit serious health issues are down to the rigorous screening of the cubs prior to attempting a return and only those fit and healthy were considered for a return.

CUBS AND DOGS

No cubs were returned following a dog removing them from within a sett. This was not influenced by a direct policy, but was based on individual circumstances excluding the consideration of a return. The retrieval of a cub by a small dog is reasonably common and I have been aware of one particular dog "offending" in two consecutive years and on one occasion retrieving two single cubs in the same year.

There are two main reasons that make these cubs a difficult group to return:

Table 8
1. Dogs can travel distances very quickly when unattended in woodland and the owners often have no idea from where the cub has originated or where the dog "found" the cub
2. The cub is often very small (pre-weaned) and injured (by the dog) and thus requiring a higher level of care or LTR

If it were possible to establish the exact location of the natal sett, then providing the cub was not injured this group would make good candidates for a potential natal return (MNR). This is providing that the dog's behaviour can be controlled.

Initially it was unclear as to the circumstances of how a dog could enter a sett and remove a cub without the sow or other badgers engaging defensively with the dog. However I have been fortunate to be able to observe adult badgers and cubs within a rescue facility. The sow does not always sleep directly with the cubs but may be in another chamber and once an adult badger is asleep they can be very difficult to awaken. It is perfectly feasible for a small dog to enter a sett (especially if the cub is rapidly keckering) and remove a cub without disturbing an adult. Cubs at 8 weeks and above become increasingly aware (defensively) of their environment and are less likely to be removed by a dog from a sett.

Although this would be difficult to prove (without DNA saliva samples from a cub's fur) I consider that small dogs may be responsible for more of these incidents of cubs found above ground than we realise. Especially those in the age range up to 7 weeks.

FINANCIAL IMPLICATIONS

The primary aim of this research was focused on animal welfare and trying to achieve the best possible outcome for cubs that are presented to a rehabilitation centre. However there are significant financial benefits in adopting a more selective and measured approach to badger cubs entering a rehabilitation centre. The costs of LTR to a rescue centre are considerable.

Over a 4 year period SWWR and a number of badger groups (liaising with SWWR and part of the research) collectively returned or supported 50 badger cubs at the natal sett. If these cubs had been entered into LTR they would have required between 7-9 release sites, all with an artificial sett. This has helped to ensure that genuine orphaned cubs entering LTR have the best release sites available. The funds that would have been used on the rehabilitation of these cubs could be directed to other animals in need of rehabilitation. It has been estimated that the cost of full LTR of a group of 6 cubs with an artificial sett is in the region of £1,500 per cub (correct as of 2015).

AGE OF RESCUED CUBS

From the case studies detailed badger cubs in the age range of 10-12 weeks old feature significantly. This is the age where cubs become more independent of the sow and they have to adjust to finding their own nutrition. If the cub's development (weaning) coincides with adverse weather then this may have an impact on the cub's ability to survive and then potentially they may be presented to a rescue centre.

THE USE OF TRAIL CAMERAS

The use of a trail camera in establishing the presence of a lactating sow or the condition of a cub post release is a very useful tool for the rehabilitator. It allows surveillance of a sett or feeding tube over long periods without the need for personal observations.

When trying to identify a sow, the positioning of the camera is crucial in obtaining clear images of the sow's underside and the presence of feeding rings.

It was found that the best images/video clips were obtained when the following points were considered:

Table 9
1. The camera is placed low down to the ground at approximately badger height and not when placed high on a tripod angled down
2. Video clips (high resolution) worked better than stills as a video can be examined in minute detail; freezing each frame as the badger changes its position
3. Placing the camera across the entrance of a sett (as opposed to head on to the entrance). As a badger exits the entrance they tend to do so slowly and with caution. A camera placed side on to the badger has a better chance of capturing the side profile/underside of the animal
4. Placing the camera (side on position) at a feeding tube or place where it is anticipated that the badgers will pause such as climbing over an object or pushing under a fence
5. If possible a camera placed against an existing object such as a tree, rock or post will help to conceal it from human interference and there is less chance of the emerging badgers treating a new object with caution

SUBORDINATE SOWS

It was noted that during the research there were significant numbers of cubs apparently deriving from subordinate sows. This observation is based on the location of where the cubs were found. It is noted that cubs found above ground during the day and in difficulties or were affected by damage to the sett could often be associated with setts in more challenging environments. It would make sense that the dominant sow within a social group would have precedence over the location to raise her cubs which would factor in a location that offered good protection, lack of disturbance and favourable habitat with water and food close by. Subordinate sows may then be left to utilise a sett which was compromised in some manner such as manure heap or an outlier sett.

AS A BROAD GUIDELINE IT CAN BE CONCLUDED:

Cub pre-weaned and not actively mobile, 1 day to approximately 8 weeks old:

Table 10
1. Generally found close to a sett
2. Generally will be from the nearest sett where found. Unless the cub has been picked up or removed from the sett, for example by a dog
3. Cubs still dependent on a sow for food must be released following a positive encounter with the sow, preferably by the sow physically picking up the cub and moving it to safety

Cub pre-weaned, 8-12 weeks:

Table 11
1. May be some distance from a sett especially in adverse weather or the sow has been killed/died Can have good sett recognition
2. Can have good sett recognition
3. Cubs still dependent on a sow for food must be released following a positive encounter with the sow or it is established that the cub has not been abandoned by the sow

Cub weaned, post 12 weeks:

Table 12
1. Often the largest group to be admitted – especially during dry weather
2. Can stray a long distance from the sett especially in adverse weather
3. Can have a good natal sett recognition
4. Should have good social bonding with other badgers in the group making a return easier (if the correct sett is located)
5. Cubs that are weaned must be returned to the natal sett or territory and establishing that the cub is in the correct location is paramount for the welfare of the cub
6. Capable of longer periods in rehabilitation before being released

In most cases it was observed that cubs found near a sett stood a reasonable chance of a natal return especially if the reason for their capture was a result of weather, disturbance or being trapped.

When surveying for a potential sett from which a cub may have originated, unless there was detailed and exceptional knowledge and access to the site a survey was not usually extended beyond 300-500m, especially if there was dense cover. It was found that the further one radiates from the place the cub was found, the data (setts/holes) obtained coupled with inaccessible areas such as gardens and sheds etc. made these returns very difficult. However, this observation is based upon surveying in the South West of England with many areas of high badger densities and numerous setts. These territories can be more compact than in other parts of the country with the risk of a cub straying into a neighbouring territory a significant concern.

There is no substitute for good local knowledge when it comes to surveying for badgers and the experience of a local badger enthusiast can be very useful.

ABANDONMENT OF CUBS (A personal perspective)

The terms used to describe a badger cub as 'orphaned' or 'abandoned' are emotive terms and whilst this does occur within badger ecology I am not convinced that the use of these terms at the initial rescue stage is advantageous to the cub's long term welfare. When a cub has been given such a label we are one step closer to admitting this cub to LTR without considering all our options.

I have witnessed experienced and caring people associated with badger rescue take a rigid stance on stopping the potential attempted release of a cub or an adult badger back to the place it was found. This is often centered on people's perceptions that the environment in which a badger has been found is one that they would not wish (from a personal perspective) to live in. Badgers are incredibly good at living amongst people and in potentially hostile environments, often going un-noticed. As badgers move into our urban or suburban environment we must respect that they have chosen to do this (albeit sometimes from the pressures of development) and where a cub return is contemplated this must be the exact place they were found. Adults brought in for treatment must also be released exactly where they were rescued. Badger cubs are orphaned naturally in the wild but unless we have initial evidence of a dead lactating sow or persecution at a sett caution should be exercised in using this term.

Abandonment is a strong term as it implies that this has been done deliberately and whilst this must happen in the wild I am not convinced this is as frequent as the term is used. Abandonment of a cub pre-weaned is a significant factor in admitting the cub for LTR. There can be many reasons a cub becomes separated from the sow or social group; see Table 1.

Before a cub is labeled as abandoned especially with smaller pre-weaned cubs (in good condition) the following points should be considered:

Table 13
1. Has the cub been removed by a small dog?
2. Could the cub have been dropped by a sow whilst moving sett?
3. Has a subordinate sow dropped the cub whilst moving to the main social group/sett?
4. Has the cub been moved by another badger or animal (poss. dominant sow moving sub-ordinate sow's cub)?

The last point may have a bearing in some cases, as adult badgers are documented exhibiting aggression against cubs and this includes infanticide. If an adult badger is capable of killing a cub then they are perfectly capable of moving and discarding this cub (unharmed) especially those belonging to a subordinate sow.

When I discovered a dead cub at a sett this was initially assumed infanticide; see Fig 27 but on reflection, this could easily have been the result of a dog or fox. This then opens up more possibilities as to how cubs become separated from the sett, some may be badly injured and others found in good condition.

If a cub is discovered in a good condition it must not automatically be assumed that the sow has abandoned this cub as there may be many influencing factors that allow an attempted natal return; including a cub that is uninjured but potentially interfered with by another badger or animal. It should be the aim of rehabilitators and those rescuing cubs to endeavor to establish as many of the facts surrounding an "orphaned/abandoned" cub, before admitting the cub into LTR.

Fig. 27

Cub dead at the sett, infanticide or dog attack?

CUBS ADMITTED FOR SHORT TERM REHABILITATION

Based upon the assumption that a natal return may be undertaken

A cub admitted to a rehabilitation centre and considered a suitable candidate for a potential release to the natal sett should always be kept in isolation from other cubs (see notes: Multiple cub releases: below) and this is centred on four issues:

Table 14
1. Cubs will scent mark each other from an early age and a cub with a scent associated with another badger from a different social group may very well be rejected by its own social group when an attempt is made to return it to the natal sett
2. There is a risk that a cub may contract a disease (e.g. parvovirus or bTB) from another cub and then in turn this could be passed on to other members of the social group when released
3. There is a significant risk of mixing up the cubs and the return of the wrong cub at a sett could have fatal consequences
4. Has the cub been moved by another badger or animal (poss. dominant sow moving subordinate sow's cub)?

MULTIPLE CUB RELEASES

When releasing two or more cubs then the above issues are still a concern and multiple cubs should be dealt with as follows:

CUBS IMMOBILE:

Cubs found together should be kept as a unit and isolated from other cubs not associated with their clan. Upon their return they should be kept together as one unit, so as to allow the sow to engage and retrieve the cubs. Scent marking within the same social group is perfectly natural.

CUBS MOBILE:

Cubs found together should be kept as one unit within the rehabilitation facility, as in all probability they will be from the same social group. If there are clinical reasons to separate the two cubs then this will be an overriding factor. Sometimes a cub is rescued and then later (day or weeks) another cub at the same location presents itself and in similar circumstances. This animal could be mixed with the first cub in the rehabilitation facility; however micro-chip marking should be used to identify each cub.

In a situation where one cub has been rescued and another is found nearby at a later date, if there are any concerns that this second cub is not a sibling or perhaps it is from a subordinate sow within the same social group, then it may be prudent to keep these two cubs separated and in isolation.

With the release of multiple cubs considered to be from the same sett it is always sensible to take the cubs to the release site together, but in separate cages. In this way the behaviour of each cub can be observed prior to and during the release. Once the cub is released, if concerns are raised based upon the behaviour of a cub it is far easier to recapture a single cub, as opposed to two or more wandering/ running off in different directions.

If one cub is quicker to respond to treatment than its sibling and if circumstances allow I would suggest releasing a cub as soon as it is ready to go. Unless the other cub is only a day or two from being considered suitable for release I would not spoil the chances of an early release of one cub over another.

If a release is unsuccessful then it may be worth considering another attempt the following night at a nearby sett associated with the social group. It is possible that the cub has not explored its immediate territory, especially if it is associated with a subordinate sow.

CHAPTER 9:
CONCLUSION

It is clear that the weather has a large bearing on the survival rates of badger cubs in the wild and during dry periods only those cubs that can access water and food will thrive. Cubs brought into a rehabilitation centre under these conditions make potentially good candidates for a return to the natal sett. This is providing the sett can be established and the cub is re-nourished and hydrated and supported with supplementary food/water during adverse weather.

During periods of dry weather adult badgers will have a good understanding of their home range and will be familiar with areas that provide food in certain seasons and during adverse weather (patch-feeding). The significance of patch-feeding is detailed within the work of Hans Kruuk [5]. Cubs will not be familiar with their wider environment and they will be reliant on following the sow and other badgers to patches of higher food concentration. In the natural environment many things can happen to a cub en route to these areas and there is great potential for the cub(s) to become lost or detached from the sow. These are the periods when cubs are vulnerable and potentially can end up in a rescue centre.

The return of badger cubs to the natal sett can be a difficult process not only in terms of the physical aspects but also from a legal/welfare perspective [2] and purely an emotional stance. Strong differences in opinions can and do emerge and at the end of the day what is best overall for the cub should be paramount. There are risks associated with LTR and the return of cubs to the natal sett; both methods having plus and minus points. People can place values and emotions on a situation that does not always have the best long term outcome for the animal concerned.

I cannot stress enough that the objections sometimes levied at not attempting to return a cub are often around ignorance or personal perspectives (emotion). What is vitally important is that sound badger ecology, a thorough site survey coupled with the cub's health status should set precedence over objections based on limited facts and excessive nurturing of badger cubs.

What has to be remembered is that just because a cub is entered into LTR this does not mean it will live a full and healthy life. The path a cub takes when it is admitted into a rescue centre can be very precarious with bTB blood testing. There is also the risk of diseases that might be acquired within a wildlife centre; Tyzzer's disease (otters Lutra lutra) [7] and parvovirus in badger cubs [8]. This is despite the very best veterinary care and standards at the centre.

There are no guarantees that a cub will be released into a new territory that will provide sanctuary and a full life; the natural world is a challenging environment and good release sites are hard to find. It is my opinion that unless there are serious and well proven reasons why an animal should not be released back to its own territory/natal sett then its early return should be the absolute priority in animal welfare.

I strongly believe that an animal released back into its own territory stands a much better chance of living a more natural life than one within a LTR programme. Every effort should be undertaken to achieve this goal. LTR and the return of badger cubs to the natal sett are equally important in terms of animal welfare. It is our responsibility as rehabilitators or rescuers to ensure that the needs of each badger cub are assessed and the appropriate release undertaken.

APPENDIX 1:
AGEING CHART

The information below is for guidance only. The weight of cubs in particular will vary according to the body condition and hydration status

Age of cub	Appearance	Eyes	Teeth	Size/ weight	Notes
At birth	Pink skin, sparse grey fur	Closed	Non	75-150g	Umbilical cord present, long and/ or wet
1 week	Pink skin, sparse grey fur	Closed	Non	200-300g	Umbilical cord dry but may still be long
5 weeks	Black and white coat	Open	Milk teeth erupting	Approx. 800g	Umbilical cord remnants gone
8 weeks	Black and white coat	Open	Milk teeth present	Approx. 1500g	Naturally seen above ground at this stage
12 weeks	Black and white coat	Open	Permanent teeth erupting	Approx. 3kg	Weaning naturally begins
15 weeks	Black and white coat	Open	Permanent teeth erupting	Approx. 5kg	Usually naturally independent

Re-produced by kind permission of Dr. Elizabeth Mullineaux MRCVS and SWWR

APPENDIX 1A:
ESTIMATING THE AGE OF BADGER CUBS: PHOTOGRAPHS

Estimating the age of a cub can be difficult as environmental and genetic factors will have a bearing on the size and development of a cub. Key indicators such as eyes open or closed and dental development (see: Appendix 1 Ageing chart) will assist in the aging a cub.

As the cub begins to wean its ability to eat solid food will become more developed. In a case where a larger cub is admitted into a rescue centre careful observations on its ability and willingness to consume and digest solid food may give some indication on its current development status i.e. partly or fully weaned.

Fig. 28

Development of "Star": 2-3 days

Fig. 29

Star: Tare weight 96.7g
3-4 days

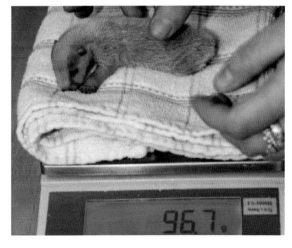

Fig: 30

Star: 3-4 days approx.
5"/12.5cm

Fig: 31

Star: Approx. 10 days

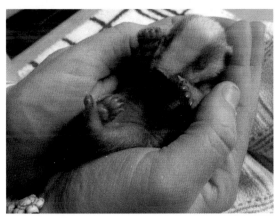

Fig: 32

Star: 7 weeks

AGE RANGE: VARIOUS CUBS:

Fig: 33

Cub: 6 days

Fig. 34

Cub: 4- 5 weeks (eyes closed)

Fig: 35

Cub: 6-7 weeks

Fig. 36

Cubs: 7-8 weeks

Fig. 37

Cub: 8- 10 weeks

Fig. 38

Cub: 12 weeks

Fig. 39

Cub: Approx. 12 weeks

APPENDIX 2:
'ORPHANED' BADGER CUB RESCUE CHECKLIST PROTOCOL & INFORMATION FORM

Recorder details/name:........................... Time:.............. Date...........

EXACT Location details:..……….

Finder details address:...…....

....…… Telephone...........................…..

Age of cub:....................... Sex:........................

This form must be completed by the person taking the call regarding the CUB and completed to the best of their ability

I. INITIAL ASSESSMENT

Is the cub showing any of the following signs?

☐ Injured ☐ Very underweight ☐ Very quiet (not whickering/keckering)

☐ Showing signs of dehydration, loose skin sunken eyes ☐ Cold to touch

☐ Lethargic ☐ In immediate danger, very public place, on a road etc.

☐ Are there any factual indications that the sow may be dead or an injury prevents the sow from attending the cub (s)

> **ANY TICKED BOXES IN THE ABOVE SECTION, ACTION: ADMIT TO WILDLIFE CENTRE/VET**
> Must have fully accurate location and contact details in case of return to sett
> Inform person responsible for orphaned cubs of this action immediately
> Please continue with rest of form

2. DEVELOPMENT OF CUB

Has the cub any of the following features:

☐ Pink colour to most of body ☐ Little or no fur present

☐ Eyes closed ☐ Cub fits easily in palm of your hand

> **ANY TICKED BOXES IN THE ABOVE SECTION, ACTION:** Cub vulnerable, consult with experienced badger cub rehabilitator/rescuer

3. IS THE CUB:

☐ Small, head/body approx. 6"- 8" (150-200mm) long (not including tail)

☐ Partly mobile but unsteady on legs due to lack of development rather than weakness or injury

☐ Found on or very near to a sett

☐ Cub looks healthy chubby appearance

☐ Fur present with distinctive black and white face markings (unless albino!)

ACTION: Contact .... Exp. rehabilitator. Consider monitored return to sett, the more ticked boxes in the above section the better

4. THE CUB IS:

☐ Mobile strong, fluid movement

☐ Size: 'bag of sugar' or larger

☐ Not necessarily found near a known sett

ACTION: CONTACT .... Experienced rehabilitator.
Consider monitored return
Consider support feed return
Consider hard release (territory found) for larger cubs later in season (following examination/treatment at Wildlife Centre)

Contact numbers: ....   :.........................

Vets.................................

Wildlife Rescue Centre:.................... ....

Action taken to resolve rescue.. ....
....
....
....
....
....
....

Parr/Cowen/SWWR

APPENDIX 3:

EMERGENCY CARE OF BADGER CUBS – NOTES FOR BADGER GROUPS

ADMISSION OF BADGER CUBS

Badger cubs must only be admitted into captivity if injured or if they are orphans genuinely at risk (see 'Badger cub rescue check list' -Appendix 2)

Admission into captivity has many risks attached to it and should only be carried out if there are no other options available.

Many cubs will be hypothermic and dehydrated and require immediate veterinary first aid at the nearest vets. All vets are legally obliged to provide emergency care to all animals and vets not confident in doing this can be directed to: (Name of Wildlife Centre) for advice. Cubs that are very young and require specialist rearing and rehabilitation and (Name of Wildlife Centre) should be contacted immediately for advice on this.

In reality the emergency medical treatment of a badger cub is no different from that of a puppy or kitten. The one difference is that badger cubs don't begin to wean until 8wks and will not eat solids properly until 10-12 weeks old.

CUBS THAT MUST SEE A VET STRAIGHT AWAY:

Cubs that are obviously injured, very underweight, very quiet (not wickering/ keckering), showing signs of dehydration (loose skin sunken eyes), cold to touch, lethargic, or that you are otherwise concerned about, must see the nearest vet straight away. In the case of other cubs the appropriate contacts can be made (see 'Badger cub rescue check list').

FIRST AID TREATMENT OF BADGER CUBS

All neonatal animals, including badger cubs, generally require food and fluids and warmth at admission. These things must however, be provided correctly and at the same time, which is not usually possible in an emergency and out of a specialist environment. If neonates are excessively warmed up without providing food and fluids (which provide glucose) they will die (of hypo-glycaemia). Equally if they are fed and fluids are provided and they not warmed correctly, they will not absorb the food or fluid adequately and will die (of hypothermia).

The main aim of emergency first aid is to stop the cub losing any more heat whilst it is moved to a place where it can be fully treated (in most instances the local vets or (Name of Wildlife Centre). The best way of doing this is to line a box (cardboard or plastic) with newspaper and cover it with a soft blanket, or fleece bedding. The cub is then placed into this with additional fleece blanket (the thin cheap sort from garages or pet shops) around the edges (for very small cubs) and lightly over the cub.

ANY ADDITIONAL CARE WILL DEPEND UPON:

• How far away you are from the vet or (Name of Wildlife Centre) – if you are within an hour (which will usually always be the case) no further treatment is required

• The age of the cub – see Ageing Chart Appendix 1

PROVISION OF HEAT TO VERY YOUNG CUBS

Cubs up to 1wk old will be very poor at controlling their own body temperature and some heat, in addition to the blankets above, can be offered if you are more than 1hr away from other help. A hot water bottle (an alternative plastic bottle with a secure lid can be used instead as necessary) covered in a thick towel can be provided, but the cub must be able to move away from this direct heat if necessary. This is best provided by having the hot bottle in one half of the box and having the cub placed next to it (not on top of it). In a clinical environment the heat source can be replaced by an incubator running at a constant heat ($28 - 30°C$).

Fluids should be provided, to cubs of all ages, before any food is given. Fluids may be oral if the cub can lift and support its own head and will feed, or may otherwise need to be given via other routes by your vet. Oral rehydration fluids should have a glucose concentration of at least 5% and/or be based upon blood glucose levels (taken by a vet). After fluid therapy a canine milk replacer is usually used at a 50% dilution (SWWR uses a product called 'Esbilac').

Re-produced by kind permission of Dr. Elizabeth Mullineaux MRCVS and SWWR

APPENDIX 4:

PROTOCOL FOR RETURNING CUBS TO THE NATAL SETT

KEY POINTS:

1. Detailed information must be collated in a consistent format: Appendix 2

2. Site survey required – Check for sow RTC , obtain as much local information as possible

3. Pre-weaned dependent cubs should only be released if a lactating sow is present and actively engaging with the cub(s). Where a sow is alive and has become temporally separated from her cub(s) due to sett destruction etc. then the sow will be given free access to the cub(s) though consideration from predation and environmental conditions must be considered

4. Weaned cubs must exhibit strong sett/environment recognition or positive encounter with an adult badger at the sett before releasing

5. Cub(s) returned should not simply be placed at a sett and left without some form of monitoring/control

6. CCTV should be used to monitor cub-sow/adult interaction

7. The use of remote release cage to be utilised where MNR is an option and there are risks of "losing" the cub prematurely

8. As part of the research, cubs wherever possible would be micro-chipped and post release monitoring with RFID after a period of at least 14 days (only for research purposes)

9. Adhere to conditions of the Government Licences

10. Adhere to good badger watching principals to cause as little disturbance as possible to badgers in the wild

11. Cubs should not be micro-chipped unless 6 weeks old (or at the discretion of a vet)

12. Welfare of the cub is paramount

13. The use of IR camera and remote monitoring to reduce disturbance to emerging adults at the sett is recommended

14. Cub must only be released if deemed fit by vet or suitably qualified person

15. All reasonable steps must be taken to protect vulnerable cub(s) especially those pre-weaned, paying particular attention to heat loss when in the open field.

16. Where cubs are admitted (and there is a potential to return to the natal sett) with an ectoparasitic burden these should be removed where possible by hand, rather than the use of a topical insecticide. This is to reduce the cub attracting a clinical odour, and the subsequent risk of the sow rejecting the cub if returned

17. If a cub is entered into rehabilitation and it is considered for a potential return this cub must remain in isolation from all other cubs in the facility (except siblings brought in together). This is to minimise disease and as cubs scent mark from a very early age a cub released into its own territory with a scent from another cub may have serious implications on its acceptance back into its social group

18. As with the return of adult badgers following rehabilitation a cub must not be released directly into a sett. The badger has to be given the option to enter a sett or move elsewhere

19. As with adult badgers entering rehabilitation a cub/adult must only be released in the immediate location they are found. Under no circumstances must any badger be released into unfamiliar territory (other than cubs as part of LTR) even if the environment perceived from a human perspective is not ideal or "perfect"

20. A cub entering a rehabilitation facility should only be released when the weather is suitable. If a sett has been positively identified then support food and water could be considered to assist an early return

21. Support food should be protected from non-target species and reduced on a diminishing basis

APPENDIX 5:

CHECKLIST FOR DEALING WITH A RESCUED BADGER CUB:

1) Information. Obtain as much information as possible prior to attending the site. Use Appendix 1 & 2 to establish age/health and whether the cub can stay on site (until surveyed) or be admitted immediately to a vet/rescue centre. Do not instruct members of the public to pick up or handle a cub without them having badger handing experience. A laypersons interpretation on the size/age of a badger may differ from yours and could result in serious injury. A mobile cub or injured adult can often be contained with an upturned bin or similar object until someone with experience can attend site

2) Attending site. Your health & safety is the priority, so assess the situation and undertake a personal risk assessment. The cub's welfare and health is the next priority; establish its health and status. You can then reassess if the cub stays on site or is admitted to a vet/rescue centre. If you are in any doubt take the cub for a veterinary examination. If the cub requires treatment then attend to this as a priority (and do not be distracted by people or site events). If there is a potential to return the cub undertake a full site survey once the cub is safe and receiving treatment, even if this means returning to the site at a later date

3) Age. Establish the age of the cub as this will determine the options for a potential return

4) Surveying the site. Your Health & Safety is paramount. Undertake a site risk assessment and only attempt what you are comfortable with. Consider the possibility of other cubs (siblings) nearby requiring assistance. Seek local knowledge and information but make a decision on what you are comfortable and trained to deal with. Look at the site and try and establish the full facts

relating to the 'abandonment' or 'orphaning'. Consider influencing factors such as: RTC (sow), poor foraging due to dry weather or excessive rain, flooding, cub trapped and the possibility of damage or interference with the sett

5) Handle the cub as little as possible and refrain from laying down excessive scent on a sett if a return is thought imminent (within 24hrs)

6) Camera. Use trail cameras to gain data

7) As a guide:
- a) Cubs that are below 2 weeks should be returned immediately. Cubs 2-8 weeks; need to be returned within a few days, 3-4 at the most
- b) Cubs that are 8-12 weeks; it is recommended that they are returned after no more than 1-2 weeks. The younger the cub the quicker they should be returned
- c) Cubs that are weaned; potentially they can be held in captivity for 2-4 weeks. Cubs that are older (16 week +) that exhibit sett recognition or social bonding with other badgers when at the sett, could be considered for release for up to 6weeks following rehabilitation

8) Returning cub. Seek veterinary advice on the cub and only attempt a release if it is deemed healthy. Undertake a risk assessment covering the cub's welfare and your site safety. If a return is considered appropriate then establish the status of the cub's dependency. Will the cub require a full MNR (pre-weaned) or can a release be attempted with cub site recognition alone? Develop an action plan based on the cub and site constraints:

Providing you undertake the release with due care and consider carefully the type of release you are proposing, you always have the fall back option of returning the cub into LTR; especially if you are unhappy with the cub or adult badgers' reaction at the release site.

GLOSSARY

BCG: Bacillus Calmette-Guérin vaccine, licenced badger vaccine against bTB

bTB: Bovine Tuberculosis (disease affecting cattle, badgers and other wild animals)

Capping: Process of protecting a sett from being dug by badger baiters, this involves concreting or burying steel mesh over the sett. The process requires a licence.

Clan: A cohesive group of badgers belonging to the same social group

Couch: A nest above ground using grass/leaves often located in quiet places and can be used during the day or night; associated with badgers and otters

CPS: Crown Prosecution Service

Ectoparasitic: Parasites (fleas/ticks) externally on the body

Feeding rings: Worn areas of hair around the nipple of a lactating animal

Feeding Tube: A pipe or vessel that food is placed within during support feeding

Grubbing up: The digging out or freeing something buried

I.R. Camera: Infrared camera, camera with the ability to view/record in total darkness

Latrine: Often a scrape in the ground where a badger defecates

LTR: Long Term Rehabilitation, process where a cub is cared for over an extended period and then released back into the wild within a new social group of similar cubs

MNR: Monitored Natal Return, process of controlling the release of an animal (badger cub) back to its natal sett

Pass-under: Where an animal (esp. badger) regularly passes under a fence or hedge creating a worn patch of ground or depression

Rapid-kecker: The rapid (machine gun type) distress calls of a cub, often referred to as a "Wail" though personally I feel the term Wail is slightly misleading

RFID: Radio Frequency Identification, Equipment that can detect and log micro-chips imbedded in animals

RTA: Road Traffic Accident

RTC: Road Traffic Collision (Accident)

Scenting the air: The process where an animal inhales and absorbs the air around its environment checking for signs of danger, food or other animals

Soft Release: Process of releasing an animal initially in an enclosure and as the animal becomes familiar with its environment it is released with support feeding

Stool: Term to describe fecal deposits

Support Feeding: Providing food for an animal within the wild usually during dry periods or when released after rehabilitation

ACKNOWLEDGEMENTS

Secret World Wildlife Rescue (Specialists in the rehabilitation of badgers) Special thanks to:

Pauline Kidner

Simon Kidner

Dr. Elizabeth Mullineaux, MRCVS

Sara Cowen, RVN BSc Hons PGCE

Martin Kendal

Laura Hawkins

For their support, contributions and in-put on field work, policies and working documents

Lancashire Badger Group:

Jo Bates-Keegan (Written contribution, editing and design)

Arlene Harris

Chris Bates-Keegan

Somerset Badger Group:

Adrian Coward (Badger ecology & advice & first-hand exp. of natal return)

Vanessa Mason

Dorset Badger Group:

Elizabeth and Derek James (RFID funding)

Uttlesford Badger Group:

Derek Barry (Written contribution)

Mid Derbyshire Badger Group:

Irene Brierton (Accounts of natal return)

Suffolk Badger Group

Adrian Hinchliffe

West Cornwall Badger Group:

Bob Speechley

Captive Animals' Protection Society (CAPS)

For the Archos recorder (Obsolete item)

REFERENCES

[1] Secret World Wildlife Rescue, National Federation of Badger Groups, Royal Society for the Prevention of Cruelty to Animals. Badger Rehabilitation Protocol: 2003

[2] Abandonment of Animals Act 1960

[3] The Protection of Badgers Act 1992

[4] http://www.wsava.org/guidelines/microchip-identification-guidelines

[5] Kruuk, Hans. (1989) The Social Badger Oxford University Press (patch-feeding) see index page 155)

[6] Neal, E. & C. Cheeseman (1996). Badgers T&A. D. Poyser. London. (Page 53/54)

[7] Simpson V R, Hargreaves J, Birtles RJ et al. (2008) Tyzzer's disease in a Eurasian otter (Lutra lutra) in Scotland. Veterinary Record 163(18), 539– 543

[8] Barlow A M, Schock A, Bradshaw J, et al. (2012) Parvovirus enteritis in Eurasian badgers (Meles meles). Veterinary Record 170(16), 416

GENERAL REFERENCES

Clark, Michael (1990) Badgers. Whittet Books

Roper, Timothy (2010) Badger. The New Naturalist Library Collins

Pearce, George (2011) Badger Behaviour Conservation & Rehabilitation: 70 Years of Getting to Know Badgers. Pelagic Publishing

Woods, Michael (2010) The Badger. (2nd Edition) The Mammal Society

INDEX

Numbers in bold indicate specific title headings

USEFUL CONTACT DETAILS

Badger Trust: www.badger.org.uk

Lancashire Badger Group: www.lancashirebadgergroup.org.uk

Secret World Wildlife Rescue: www.secretworld.org

Somerset Badger Group: www.somersetbadgers.org.uk

Badgerland: www.badgerland.co.uk

Captive Animals' Protection Society: www.captiveanimals.org